RHODES

the brilliant island of the sun

EDITIONS
TOUBI'S ®
ΕΚΔΟΣΕΙΣ

© Copyright   MICHAEL TOUBIS PUBLICATIONS S.A.
                   Nisiza Karela, Koropi, Attiki.
                   Telephone: +30 210 6029974, Fax: +30 210 6646856
                   Web Site: http://www.toubis.gr

ISBN: 960-540-148-7

"*The island of Rhodes opened like a flower from the watery depths,
child of Aphrodite, Goddess of Love,
and then became the bride of the Sun*"

Pindar

At bottom the relationship one has with Rhodes is based on love. It is not by chance that the goddess Aphrodite emerged from its waters and her beautiful little statue can be seen in the island's Archaeological Museum, the old Hospital of the Knights of St. John. Down through time this relationship based on love has always developed between the island, its inhabitants and its visitors. The golden sun, the dark blue sea and bougainvilleas, the hibiscus, the medieval town, the lush green landscape, the imposing Palace of the Grand Masters, the villas with their jasmine, the new market with its cosmopolitan flavor and its up-to-the minute shops will stay indelibly etched on your memory. Above all else there is the Old Town, Rhodini, Paradeisi, the famed Valley of the Butterflies, verdant landscapes, meadows in full flower together with the complex of hotels which is the best in Greece. What should you praise first? The deer at Tafro, the ships of every shape and size that crowd Mandraki and the main harbor, the cruise ships that ceaselessly come and go, the daily boats plying the sea between Symi and Rhodes, the waves breaking against the rocks of Neoreio? But what would all these be worth if there was not the living artistic and intellectual tradition of the island? The church of the Annunciation with paintings by Kontoglou, the picture gallery with representative works of all the great modern Greek painters, the exhibition hall with its unique collection of Byzantine and post-Byzantine art, the theaters, the concerts, the library with its archives for historical research. And just think of all the people who have passed through this unparalleled corner of Greece, both Greeks and foreigners. They have all left traces of their passage. Both here and in Kameiros and Lindos. The only way to complete you knowledge of the island is by reaching its other end at Ayios Pavlos, "St. Paul". There is a long-held tradition that the Apostle Paul, who consolidated Christianity, also stopped here. Gennadi which I knew as a fishing village has today developed into a coastal town. Then there is Attavyros, the sturdy and "stout-hearted mountain", the villages with their picturesque manners and customs, Archangelos, Ebonas, Afantou and all the others. How many battles were fought so that this land could remain Greek and its inhabitants Orthodox? And under the most adverse conditions. All Rhodes is like a painting. It would be a shame not to place your foot on its Eros-imbued soil and make it your own.

I. M. CHATZIFOTIS

CONTENTS

CONTENTS

1

RHODES

The Island of the Sun
Origin and Name - Geographical Framework

The origin of Rhodes is connected to a myth mentioned by Pindar. According to that myth, when Zeus defeated the Giants and became lord and master of the Earth, he decided to divide it up among the Olympian gods. But during this division Helios, the Sun-God, was absent and "no one remembered to include him in the draw and thus this purest of the gods was left without a country of his own". When Helios returned he complained to Zeus about the injustice that had been done to him and he asked the father of the gods to promise him that the land that would come forth from the sea would become his. And indeed while he was speaking, a beautiful, flower-strewn island began to slowly merge from the deep blue sea. It was Rhodes. Overcome with happiness Helios bathed the island in his own radiance and made it the loveliest island in the Aegean Sea.

Another myth attributes the origin of Rhodes to the love Helios had for the nymph Rhodos, who was the daughter of Poseidon, the god of the sea. When he saw her, as the myth tells us, Helios was so smitten by her beauty that he made her his wife. Together they had one daughter and seven sons. According to the myth, one of their sons, Kerkafos, had three children: Kameiros, Ialyssos and Lindos who built the three largest towns on the island. It is also said that the island took its name from the nymph Rhodos alone, while another source says the name comes from Greek word for rose. On this island of myths and flowers, the centuries have left the marks of a flourishing and rich culture. Its geographical position has played an important role in the develop of the island's commerce, even in prehistoric times and it has provided it with long periods of prosperity throughout its three thousand year long history.

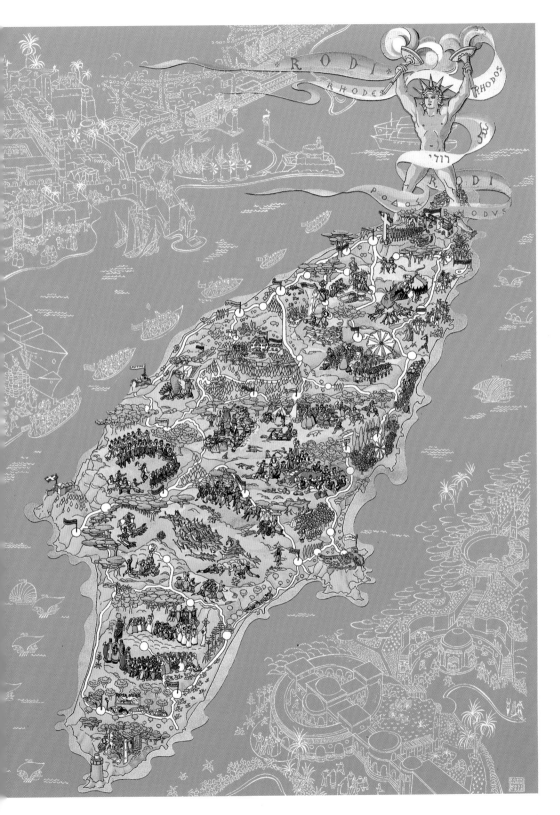

11

Rhodes, the pearl of the Mediterranean, as it has been called, is of enormous interest both for its natural beauties and for its archaeological treasures. That is the reason UNESCO recently proclaimed it a monument of global cultural heritage. With its marvellous climate and excellent tourist infrastructure it is suitable for holidays year round.
Rhodes receives visitors from all parts of the world. They come here to admire its archaeological sites, to wander through its natural beauties and to enjoy the clean water of its sea which sparkles under the rays of a "brilliant sun".

Enormous sand beaches, picturesque harbors, a sea of impressive depth, crystal-clear springs, deeply-shaded valleys, green mountains, monuments from all periods, dazzling white villages and the good-hearted islanders themselves are the main hallmarks of this beautiful land.

In the ravishing "Valley of the Butterflies" one can confirm for himself just how much beauty and harmony it is possible for a person to enjoy when he has enough sensitivity to complement and underline the natural grandeur of a place. Just outside the town of Rhodes lies Rhodini Park in a dark green ravine. Peacocks live and breed there. Near its eastern end lies the gorgeous Epta Piges ("Seven Springs") that supply an artificial lake with their water. There are medicinal springs on Rhodes, lying in a superb natural environment at the coastal site of Kallithea. The mountain of Profitis Ilias is thought to be the oldest refuge for the Rhodian deer. At its foot is the "Nymfi" spring, which supplies the town of Rhodes with water. Blessed with abundant sun and endowed with fertile soil, Rhodes produces some of the finest fruits and vegetables in the Mediterranean. Vineyards are cultivated in many places and they produce the famed fragrant wine of Rhodes.

The emerald isle of Rhodes lies in the southeastern part of the Aegean sea on the sea lane between East and West. It is the largest island there and the capital of a complex of approximately two hundred other islands known as the Dodecanese. Several of these, including Rhodes itself, broke through the surface of the sea in the distant past as a result of earthquakes. The fossilized seashells on the slopes of the mountains confirm this and add substance to the myth of Rhodes' birth.

Rhodes lies 270 nautical miles from Piraeus and is surrounded by the islands of Symi, Tilos, Chalki and Alimia as well as the rocky outcroppings of Tragousa, Makry, Strongyli, Drosonisi, Prasonisi, Galouni and Tetrapoli.

It has an area of 1,400 sq. km., a length of 78 km. and a width of 38 km. at its widest point. Its coastline has a length of 220 km. consisting primarily of level sand beaches split by steep cliffs. The southernmost point of the island is found at Prasonisl which is joined to the island by a strip of sand. The land is by and large mountainous, with small plains, verdant ravines and river-beds, valleys and plateaus. The highest mountain is Attavyros (1,215 m.) with the smaller mountains of Akramytis (825 m.) and Profitis Ilias (798 m.).

Rhodes has, on an average, 300 days of sunshine a year. The continual sunshine and the mild climate make the island suitable for viticulture.

Its superb climate, the fertile soil and the geographical position are the main factors which have made the island densely populated from antiquity up to the present. Its population today is around 90,000 and they are able to play host to more than 1,250,000 visitors a year. Visitors who come to enjoy the island's natural beauty and to get acquainted with its long history.

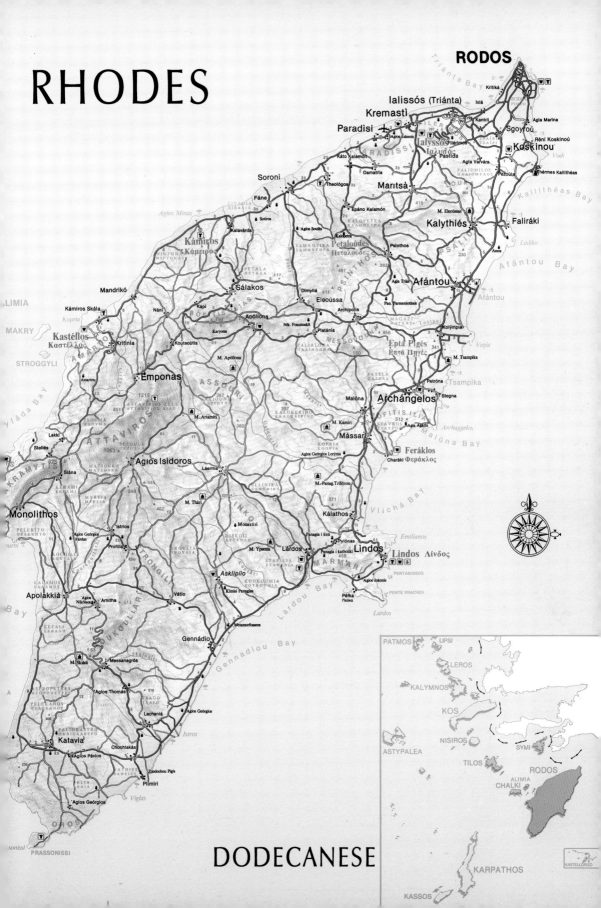

HISTORY

Prehistory - Classical Antiquity - The Roman Period Byzantium and the Middle Ages - Modern Times

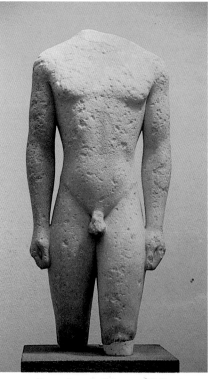

Kouros from the 6th century B.C.

The history of Rhodes, like the rest of Greece, has its beginnings in the murky depths of myth. During this mythical period it was occupied by the Telchines, a strange race said to be endowed with magical powers. The Telchines, considered by many to be demons, were, outside everything else, gifted metal-workers. They made the "harpi" the fearful sickle-shaped sword of Chronos, and Poseidon's trident as well. It is also said that they made the first bronze statues of the Olympian gods. The Telchines were driven from Rhodes by the Heliads, the children of Helios and the nymph Rhodos. The first real inhabitants of the island are thought to have been the Carians, a people from Asia Minor opposite. The Carians were followed by the Phoenicians who made Rhodes into an important commercial center. Cadmus established the first colony of Phoenicians there and he also introduced the first alphabet. But it was when Minoan Crete set up its own colony there that Rhodes got the chance to make its appearance in the history of the Eastern Mediterranean. The Minoans lived there in peace for many centuries until new colonists arrived on the island. These were the Greek Achaeans from Mycenae, Tiryns, Argos and Attica. After they had settled in their new homeland by around 1400 B.C. they set up a powerful state which soon expanded to neighboring Asia Minor. The Achaeans were in turn followed some centuries later by the warlike Dorians who overran Rhodes where they developed the towns of Lindos, Ialyssos and Kameiros which acquired great power and wealth.

The Rhodians led by Tlepolemos, the son of Hercules, took part in the Trojan War with nine ships. The leader, however, of the "imperious Rhodians" was killed in battle before the walls of Troy, along with Sarpidon.

From 1000 to 600 B.C. the three largest towns on the island, Kameiros, Ialyssos and, above all, Lindos founded many colonies on the shores of Asia Minor, Sicily, France and Spain.

Head of Helios, 2nd century B.C. the Archaeological Museum of Rhodes.

Classical Antiquity

The three above-mentioned towns retained their administrative independence at first but later joined with the other Doric towns of Kos, Knidos and Halicarnassus to form the so-called "Doric Heaxpolis" a league of six towns with a political and religious character which had its seat at the sanctuary of Apollo Triopios near Knidos.

In the 5th and 4th century Rhodes fell under the influence of the Persians together with Ionia and the rest of the coast of Asia Minor. The Persians left when the Greeks waged successful wars against them. Rhodes then became a part of the Delian League under Athenian leadership. Later, and throughout the Peloponnesian War, the Rhodians were at times under the influence of the Athenians and other times the Spartans, but finally sided with the latter.

While the Peloponnesian War was still in progress, and for reasons of greater security, the Rhodians decided to found a new town and so the three largest towns on the island joined together to create a new one. Thus at the initiative of Dorieas, son of the Olympic victor Diagoras, the new capital was established on the northeastern tip of the island and given the name Rhodes. Its founding, in 408 B.C. proved to be a landmark in the history of the island.

The town, as beautiful as the island itself, was sometimes under the influence of Athens and sometimes Sparta until the role of Macedonia in Greek affairs came to the fore. The Rhodians sided with the Macedonians and allowed them to establish a Macedonian garrison in the town. Later, during the siege of Tyre, they helped Alexander the Great conquer it.

With the dismemberment of the empire of Alexander the Great, Rhodes developed close commercial and political ties with the Egyptian Ptolemies which the King of Syria, Antigonos, did not look upon at all favorably because these ties signified to him that Rhodes would ally itself with Egypt in the war he was planning on declaring against the latter.

Female head, 4th cent. B.C., Archaeol.Museum of Rhodes.

Thus is the summer of 305 B.C. he sent his son, Dimitrios Poliorkitis ("The Besieger") to capture the town of Rhodes.

Despite the Besieger's numerical superiority, the Rhodians managed to resist for an entire year and to force Dimitrios to lift his siege. The great general left Rhodes in shame, leaving his famous siege equipment behind. The Rhodians later sold this equipment in order to built the famous Colossus, the enormous bronze statue of the god Helios, as a symbol of their gratitude to the gods.

After the destruction of Tyre, Rhodes reached unheard of heights. The failure of Poliorkitis to weaken the island's power marked the beginning of a new era for Rhodes until its trade and maritime activities reached peaks that practically no town had ever achieved before. The Rhodians put into application the "Rhodian Naval Code", a code of international law, considered to be one the most important legal documents in the world.

The emperor Antonios wrote of the Rhodian Naval Code with great admiration: "We may rule the world but the Rhodian Code rules the seas".

The Roman Period

The intervention of Rome in the affairs of Greece and the Eastern Mediterranean became increasingly perceptible by the end of the 3rd century B.C. The Rhodians, doing their best to benefit from this new situation, maintained a friendly stance toward the Romans. But the Romans were far more interested in limiting Rhodes' power and declared Delos a free port. This was a death blow for Rhodian commerce. Utterly defeated economically it was forced to come to an agreement which obliged it to have the same friends and enemies as Rome. This had disastrous consequences for Rhodes. The final blow came from Cassius. After the assassination of Julius Caesar, the Rhodians refused to give help to Caesar's enemies. Enraged, Cassius captured Rhodes on 42 B.C. and destroyed it with incredible savagery, transferring to Rome 3,000 of its artistic masterpieces.

*View of Rhodes from the port
(Flandin, l'Orient 1853).*

Byzantium and the Middle Ages

Rhodes, as a major commercial link between East and West, quickly responded to the new ideas of Christianity. Tradition says that St. Paul preached the new religion at Lindos in 58 B.C. and that many converted to Christianity. By the 1st century B.C. Rhodes already had a Metropolitan, Prochoros, who was succeeded by Foteionos and Euphranoras, the latter taking part in the First Ecumenical Council at Nicea. After the division of the Roman Empire Rhodes became capital of the Byzantine Province of the Islands. It was thus prey to the fortunes and the vicissitudes of the Byzantine Empire and was subject to frequent conquest and destruction. For example, in 620 A.D. it was occupied by the Persians under Chosroes. In 651 the Saracans appeared and it 807 it was plundered by the fleet of the Caliph Haroun-El-Raschid. Rhodes was once more sacked, this time by pirates, at the end of the 12th century when Alexios I was emperor of Byzantium. In the 11th century Rhodes began to have direct contacts with the West again. In 1082, the Venetians received the permission of the emperor to set up a commercial station in the harbour.

St. Lucia. 14th century (Blessed Virgin of the Castle).

In 1191 Richard the Lionhearted of England and King Philip of France came to Rhodes with their fleet to enlist mercenaries for the Crusades.

When the Crusaders occupied Constantinople in 1204, a local landowner, Leon Gavalas, declared himself the ruler of Rhodes, with the consent of the Venetians.

When the Byzantine Empire regained control of Constantinople in 1261 Rhodes was formally a part of that empire once more, but in actual fact remained in the hands of the Genoese admirals who were in its harbor. In 1306, one of these admirals, Vignolo Vignoli, sold it along with Kos and Leros sold it to the Order of the Knights of Saint John of Jerusalem who took full control of the island in 1309 after the fierce opposition of the Rhodians (See the chapter on the Knights of Rhodes). The Knights remained on Rhodes for 213 years until 1522 when the last Grand Master was forced to hand over the town to the Turkish sultan Suleiman.

The Turkish occupation of Rhodes was certainly the darkest period of its history. The island was under the jurisdiction of the Kapudan Pasha (Admiral of the Fleet) while the town itself was established the capital of the Vilayet (Province) of the Aegean and seat of the General Governor. The Greek inhabitants were forced to leave the walled town and settle outside it where they formed new neighborhoods called "marasia". Despite that, the Turks were never ever able to dominate the island and the Turkish population was a great deal smaller than the Greek. The Greeks took trade into their own hands, sending their many merchant ships as far as Europe. During that dark time of foreign occupation many towns, and Lindos in particular, were able to flourish due to their trade in foodstuffs, clothing, silver, household goods and perfumes. Lindos also developed into a center for light industry.

Crucifixion (16th century, Ayios Spyridonas).

Modern Times

The Turks remained in Rhodes, and the rest of the Dodecanese, until 1912. In that year the Italians, with the assistance of the island's Greek inhabitants, were able to capture Rhodes. At first the Italians treated the local population with understanding and the Rhodians hoped to be quickly united with Greece. But the rise of fascism in Italy led to expansionist policies and the Rhodians were denied the right to self-determination. This led to the outbreak of intense resistance against the foreigner conqueror. After the defeat of the Axis, Rhodes, like the remainder of the Dodecanese, came under British administration until 7 March, 1948 when the Greek flag was raised over the Governor's Palace.

The Governor's Palace and the interior of the courtyard along the town's coast. The Greek flag was raised her in March 1948.

3

THE KNIGHTS OF RHODES

The Period of the Knights from 1309 to 1522
The palaces - The walls - The organization of the Knights

The Period of the Knights

The years when Rhodes was occupied by the Order of the Knights of St. John could be consider as one of Rhodes' most flourishing periods. The Order had been founded as a philanthropic brotherhood in Jerusalem by merchants from Amalfi, Italy who were permanent residents of the Holy Lands. In time and particularly after 1099 when the Crusaders occupied Jerusalem, the Order gained considerable strength and took on the character of a military body under the control and the authority of the Church.

After the capture of Jerusalem by Saladin in 1187 the Knights shifted their base to Acre in northern Palestine, then to Ptolemais and finally to Cyprus where King Henry II ceded Limassol to them. They remained on Cyprus for only 18 years and then settled on Rhodes in 1309 after overcoming the inhabitants' heroic resistance.

The years that the Knights lived on Rhodes were the

A fully-armed knight at prayer. (Relief tombstone).

most brilliant in their history. Immediately after completing their domination of the island, the Order of the "Knights of St. John of Jerusalem", which was now called The Order of the "Knights of Rhodes" conquered the surrounding islands and also held Smyrna for a long period. They stayed on Rhodes for 213 years, that is until 1522 when on 29 December the last Grand Master Philip Villiers de l'Isle Adam was forced to hand over the town to the Sultan Suleiman the Magnificent. The surrender occurred only after six months of siege and the stiff resistance of the Knights who were assisted by the Greek inhabitants of the island. After the fall of Rhodes the Knights settled on Malta with the assistance of Charles V (1530) and the Pope and from then on were called the Knights of Malta. The Knights left imposing evidence of their time on Rhodes and gave it its particular color which the town still retains in its impregnable walls, its gates, the churches and the hospitals, the inns and the majestic palaces.

The town of Rhodes from a 15th century drawing.

The coats-of-arms of the various Langues:

France - Auvergne

Provence

Portugal

Germany

Navarre

Aragon

Castille

The Organization of the Knights

The Order of Knights had three categories of members:

a) The "Knights" themselves with military duties; they never exceeded six hundred in number and they had to be descended from noble families.

b) The "Chaplains" who were the priests and performed the religious functions of the order.

c) The "Serving Brothers" who assisted the Knights in war and administration and also acted as male nurses for the care and the treatment of the ill. The "Chaplains" and the "Serving Brothers" did not have to be of noble origins but they had to have been born of free men and not slaves.

Its members, which came from all the Catholic countries of Europe, were arranged into seven national and linguistic groups called "Langues" (tongues or "languages"). These were: Provence, Auvergne, France, Italy, England, German and Spain which later split into two: Aragon and Castille.

Each Langue stayed in its own "Inn" along with its leader and his Council. Overall government was controlled by the Grand Master who was elected for life by the members of the Order. A Council, with legislative and disciplinary powers, assisted him in his administration; these were the leaders of each Langue. The official language of the order for all its documents was Latin while French was used for oral communication.

The Langue of France which usually enjoyed the support of the Langues of Provence and Auvergne was in the majority and of the 19 Grand Masters who ruled Rhodes for the 213 years the Order was there, fourteen were French. This is also evident from the names that accompany the coats-of-arms.

Gates in the Walls of the Knights:

Above left: The grand Amboise Gate was built in 1512 by the Grand Master d'Amboise and lies on the northwest side of the medieval town. Right: St. Paul's Gate next to the Gate of Liberation on the northeast side of the Knights' town. Below: The Gate of St. John or Koskinou from 1457 with the coats-of-arms of the Grand Masters on the south side of the town.

CULTURE & TRADITION

Literature & Arts - The Colossus - Manners and Customs
Occupations - Architecture - Cultural Events

The entire atmosphere one finds on Rhodes bears witness to a refined aesthetics and a highly developed cultural sensibility. Since antiquity Rhodians have been adept at literature and the arts. The world famous Colossus was considered one of the seven wonders of the ancient world. The cosmopolitan atmosphere the rules the island and the influences that it has received from tourism have not changed the Rhodian character. Polite and hospitable, pleasure-loving and sociable, the people have managed to attract visitors to nearly all of their events. Many of their customs and manners have been revived with the participation of foreigners, mainly those that take place in the countryside. The architecture on the island is based on a number of different periods and culture. Entering the town of Rhodes you have the feeling you are suspended in time. The echoes of antiquity are combined with memories of Byzantium and the time of the Knights and amid all these remembrances of past centuries one also finds the signs of contemporary life.

Literature

Rhodes had already developed into an important center for literature and the arts in antiquity. After the 3rd century B.C. it became a true university where not only locals studied but young men from all parts of the then known world. Distinguished Romans such as Cicero, Julius Caesar, Lucretius, Pompey, Tiberius and Cassius all came to Rhodes to learn the art of rhetoric and to study philosophy.

Peisandros from Kameiros distinguished himself in epic poetry and in his famous poem "Heraclea" he praises the achievements and virtues of the mythical hero. Antagoras, from the town of Rhodes, wrote an epic entitled "Thebais" and some inscriptions. The Alexandrian poet Apollonius (295-215 B.C.), known as "Apollonius of Rhodes", lived and worked in Rhodes where he was the greatest epic poet of the Alexandrian period. The best-known of his works is "The Voyage of Argo". Of the philosophers, the Lindian Cleobuline stands out along with the Stoic philosopher Panaetios. The great sage Cleobulos, was born in Lindos in the 7th century B.C. and lived there. The son of Euagoras, he was a wise law-giver and a far-sighted politician who ruled his home town for forty years. Many maxims are attributed to Cleobulos among which are moderation in all "things", "keep sensuous pleasure in tight control", "mind makes the leader" and "avoid wrong-doing". Among Rhodian historians mention is made of Polyzelos, Zeno, Antisthenes, Poseidonios, Kallixenos, Sosicrates and others.

Rhetoric was the pride of Rhodes. Its School, founded in 324 B.C. by the Athenian orator Aeschines, gathered students from throughout the Mediterranean basin, from Rome in particular. Among the famous orators mentioned are Molon, Apollonius, Poseidonios, Menecles and Archelaos. The great Cicero had this to say in respect to Molon: "I came to Rhodes to attend Molon's rhetoric lessons. He is a gifted orator and excellent writer with a finely-honed judgement. He lectures with wisdom and his lessons have achieved the success they deserve".

The Arts

Rhodes flourished in the arts as much as it did in literature. Sculpture, painting and pottery produced works whose quality and numbers still continue to astound us. The best known of the sculptors were Chares, Philiskos, Aristonidas, the brothers Apollonios and Tauriskos, as well as Agesandros, Athenodoros and Polydoros. The Lindian Chares, a student of Lysippos, made the famous Colossus, one of the seven wonders of the ancient world.

Philiskos was the creator of statues of Apollo, Leto, Artemis and the Muses. Aristonidas worked with exceptional skill on the bronze statue of the grieving Athamas. who in a moment of madness killed his son, Learchos. The brothers Apollonios and Tauriskos, who spent most of their time in Rhodes, made the famous composition called the "Farnese Bull" (there is a replica in the museum of Naples). The best known work of the three sculptors Agesandros, Athenodoros and Polydoros is the Laocoon. This exceptional work of art depicts the punishment of the priest of Apollo, Laocoon, who for the disrespect he showed the god was condemned, along with his children, to die in the deadly grip of two enormous snakes that the god has called forth from the sea. This famous group was transferred to Rome in the 1st century A.D. and was found, in 1506, near the baths of Nero's palace. Pliny, who makes mention of it, thought it to be the supreme work of sculpture or painting, while today it is included among the masterpieces of Greek art.

Copy of the famous Laocoon group which ornaments the room in Castello bearing the same name.

Along with sculpture painting was also cultivated on Rhodes. Many of the sculptors were also painters. But the greatest Rhodian painter, as well as one of the most important in all of ancient Greece, was Protogenes.

Among the outstanding works produced by Protogenes were Ialyssos with his hunting dog, the Resting Satyr and Tlepolemos, while the Propylaea of the Acropolis in Athens bear his famous composition of two Attican triremes, the Paralos and Ammonias.

Pottery also flourished on Rhodes. The elegant pots from Ialyssos and Kameiros, distinguished for the delicacy of their representations, were already famous during the Minoan period. From 1500 B.C. until 700 B.C. Rhodian pottery depicted, with astonishing skill, mythological motifs of scenes taken from the Homeric epics. The cups and cylixes of this period were called "Rhodian" by the ancients. But Rhodian ceramics truly came to the fore after the decline of Athenian pottery-making toward the end of the 4th century B.C.

Black-figured Attican hydria (Archaeol. Museum of Rhodes).

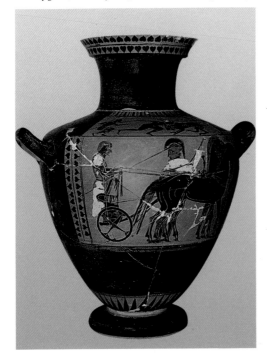

The Colossus

The world-famous Colossus of Rhodes is connected to the siege of the town by Dimitrios the Besieger in 305 B.C. Proud of their great victory the Rhodians decided with the funds they raised from the sale of Dimitrios' siege equipment to erect a triumphal statue to their great god, Helios. The work was assigned to Chares of Lindos who worked on it for twelve years (304 to 292 B.C.)

Despite the fact the Colossus was considered one of the seven wonders of the ancient world, both a technical and artistic masterpiece, there is a lack of vital information concerning the site it occupied and its actual shape. It is calculated to have been about 31 meters high. It is said that Chares cast the bronze limbs of the statue very slowly, on the spot, within enormous mounds of earth., moving from the bottom upward, just as one would build a house.

According to one account, the Colossus stood across the entrance to the harbor allowing ships to pass between its open legs. Today it is almost certain it stood on dry land and that the most likely site was the enclosure of the temple of Helios, near the palace of the Grand Masters. But this "wonder" stood for no more than 66 years. During a severe earthquake in 266 B.C. it cracked at the knees and fell. The Rhodians, fearing a curse, did not reerect it and it lay there in a heap for many centuries.

But in 653 A.D. when the Arabs of Moab pillaged Rhodes, they sold the pieces to a Jewish merchant. Tradition says that it took 900 camels to transport it. But the legend surrounding it was so closely tied to Rhodes, that for many centuries both Greeks and Westerners called the Rhodian people "Colossians".

This most extraordinary representation of thr Colossus was done by the French traveller Rotiers in 1826.

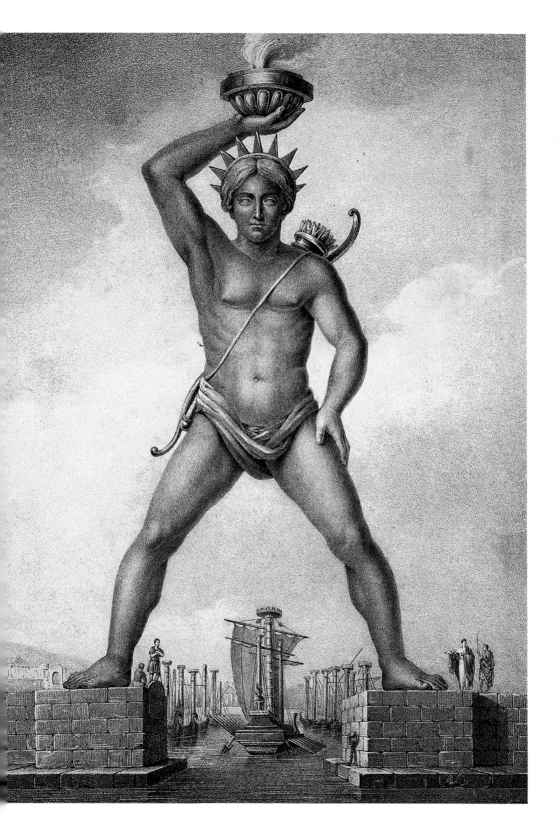

Manners and Customs

The island is imbued with a cosmopolitan atmosphere. Despite the fact that the islanders have received almost constant influence from foreign visitors this has not changed them. They have remained uncomplicated, kind-hearted and hospitable. Their intelligence and their business acumen have led to economic development but this has not influenced their behavior, either toward their fellow islanders or tourists. Polite, sociable and comfortable in their relationships with foreigners, they have a deep love for their island and do whatever they can to make sure the travellers take away a good impression. Perhaps one would not be able to discern these features at once during the height of the tourist season but it is certain they do exist; it is just that the opportunity might not arise to discover them.

Rhodians are merrymakers, shown by the number of dances and festivals they organize. No opportunity goes unexploited. Sometimes it is the feast-day of a saint, sometimes the major holidays of the year, sometimes a joyous anniversary, other times some happy event; they all supply an excuse for merrymaking and dancing which even draws in spectators during the height of the festivities.

The major Christian holidays, (Easter, Christmas, the Epiphany, the Ascension of the Virgin Mary), are all celebrated with particular magnificence. All of the smaller festivals and feasts take on a more intense feel in the Rhodian countryside.

An inseparable part of every feast is the famed Rhodian wine. This wine has been renowned since antiquity. During the Middle Ages the Knights of St. John contributed to the knowledge of this fine wine, a process which still goes on today. Most of the growers who sell their grapes to the producers, also make their own wine according to their own individual method. Often, when they have put aside enough for their own consumption, they sell the rest to the island's cafes and tavernas.

Occupations

Up until the Middle Ages Rhodes was a great naval power. Most of its inhabitants were merchants or sailors. The Turkish occupation that followed was a difficult period for Rhodians. They were obliged to move to areas outside the town but slowly, and after having taken commerce into their own hands, they contributed to the creation of economic prosperity, something rare for that period. As the years went by economic activity grew less brisk. The inhabitants turned more and more to farming and animal husbandry. Since 1950 these too have been steadily abandoned as the population tuned toward tourism.

Today most of the inhabitants are occupied first and foremost with professions that are connected to tourism and commerce. Of course there are still some who remain true to the rural life and are involved with farming, animal husbandry, viticulture, fishing and beekeeping. There are still others who are employed at the traditional crafts: embroidery, weaving, carpet-making, pottery-making and ceramics. The famous and still highly sought Lindian plates have been produced since the 16th century. They are characterized by a profusion of compositions with the dominant element being representations from nature, (deer, fish and birds in particular) all in marvellous combinations crafted with incomparable charm and expertise.

The famous stone plates still decorate Rhodian houses.

Architecture

The sensitivity and good taste which is evident in these forms of folk art, find their highest expression in Rhodian dwellings. Their architecture is based on elements taken from various period and cultures. Here one can spot the tendencies and the characteristics of island folk culture, but at the same time there are influences from western and eastern styles, which were bound to be brought to the island by the wide variety of its conquerors and visitors. The simple folk houses where the farmers live, the houses of the middle class, the towers and the mansions of Lindos are all examples of the trends that at some point held sway in the fashioning of the island's architectural identity.

Characteristic picturesque architectural details are the various decorative features on the town's dwellings. The old reliefs, damaged by time, bear witness to the concern and the aesthetics of other centuries. Decorative designs, groups, mythological representations and coats-of-arms have been set down on stone surfaces and have been incorporated into various architectural members. Even the carved marble fountains that ornament the streets and the squares demonstrate the sensitivity and good taste of the Rhodians.

Modern Rhodian houses have kept the features of traditional architecture alive. Stone paved courtyards, "hayiatia" (a kind of enclosed balcony) supported on and decorated with arches, the white and colored surfaces of walls, boldly painted doors and windows and folk decorative features are what dominate in a polychrome environment of greenery and flowers.

Startling compositions and a refined sense of harmony have also left their mark on the modern houses of Lindos. They have entire sides decorated with reliefs or inlaid elements.

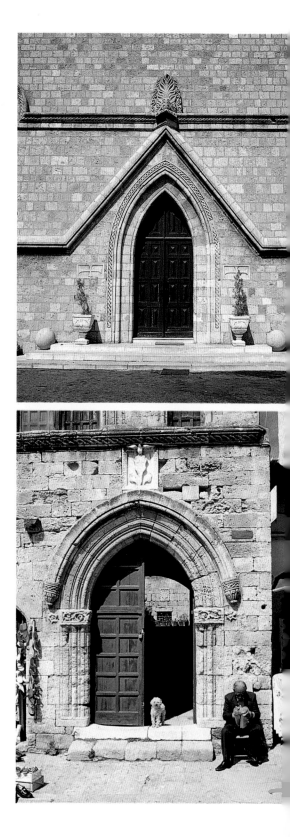

Cultural Events

Cultural activity is intense and there are a number of organized concerts, theatrical performances and exhibitions, particularly during the summer months.

During the winter the island scene changes somewhat. This is when the accounts for the year are drawn up and future plans put into perspective. The days move at a calm pace. Life is peaceful. This is truly a different period for one to get to know the island. It is for those who want peace and quiet and would like enjoy the variety of the island's natural beauties. Even during the winter there are frequent conferences and seminars, global in scope, because the island has modern installations and the up-to-the-minute technological means with which to organize them.

But whatever season one decides to visit Rhodes it is certain that he will be entranced by the beauty of its landscape and the gentility of its people. It is amazing how the entire atmosphere gives the feeling of the companionship supplied by all the peoples that have passed through the island and have left a piece of their life, each one thus contributing in his own way to its history and its culture.

It is certain that everyone will bid adieu to the island with the best impressions imprinted on his mind and it is certain that he will want to reexperience the nobility of its atmosphere.

The holding of conferences, concerts, theatrical performances, exhibitions as well as a number of feasts are but of the cultural events that are held in Rhodes even in winter.

Reading the words "Medieval Town" one should not imagine that he is going to a dead town to see ruined monuments. This is a vital town with approximately 6,000 residents who live and work in the same buildings where the Knights of St. John lived nearly six centuries ago: a living monument, one of the few in Europe, if not the world. Even if you only visit Rhodes for a few hours you should not neglect making at least a brief tour.

The **town around the castle** was divided, as it is today, into two parts: the northern, which was called the Collachium and the southern, and larger one, called Chora or Bourgo.

An interior wall divided the two sections. Lachitos St. now runs through the gate that permitted communication between the Collachium and Chora.

The northern section was and is dominated by the Palace of the Grand Masters, the well-known Castello, the acropolis of the Knights. The Collachium also contains the official churches of the Order, as well as the Knights' apartments. During the time of the Knights the southern section of the town, Chora, was called Bourgo. Besides the Greeks, other people of various nationalities lived and worked there.

The center of economic activity in the medieval town was located in the market which traversed the present streets of Apollonion and Sokratous and reached the Marine Gate. The town was surrounded by its famed gardens, the most impressive that of the Palace of the Grand Masters.

Aerial view of the medieval town.

TOWN Castello - the Collachium - Chora - the Walls

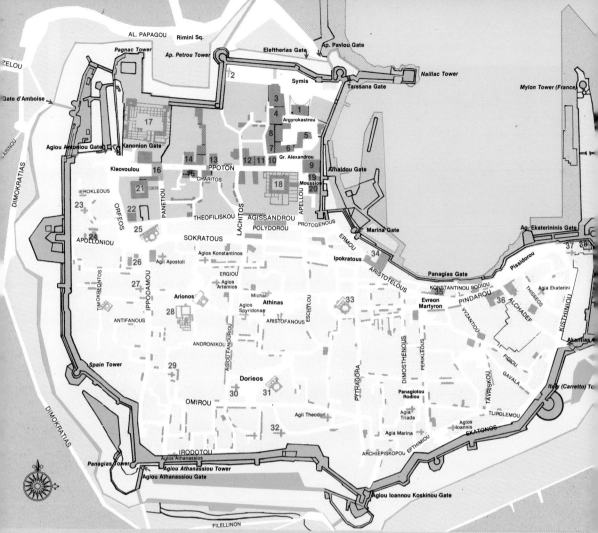

Legend of the Medieval Town

Collachium (Castello)

1. The Temple of Aphrodite
2. Saint Dimitrios
3. Gallery
4. Ionian Bank
5. Inn of Auvergne
6. Folklore Museum
7. Archaeological Museum
8. Jewellery Collection

9. The Blessed Virgin of the Castle
10. Inn of Italy
11. Small Palace
12. Inn of France
13. Holy Trinity
14. Inn of Provence
15. Inn of Spain
16. Loggia of St. John

17. Palace of the Grand Masters
18. Archaeological Museum
    Hospital of the Knights
19. National Bank of Greece
20. Inn of England
21. Turkish School
22. Clock Tower

Chora or Bourgo

23. Saint Mark
24. Monastery of Ayios Georgios
25. Suleiman Mosque
26. Turkish Library
27. Ayia Paraskevi
28. Mustapha Baths
29. Saint Nikolaos
30. Ayios Fanourios

31. Radjep Pasha Mosque
32. Ayia Kyriaki
33. Ibrahiim Pasha Mosque
34. Castellania
35. The Admiralty
36. Our Lady of the Town
37. Ayios Panteleimonas
38. Our Lady of Victory

*Time has left its mar
on he countless rooms
and walls of the old buildings.
The curved shapeand openings,
the traditional buildings
and the narrow lanes are allimages
of old, times different vudtomd,
other feelings and another way of life.*

The Knights' Castle *(Collachium)*

Setting off from Mandraki harbor your enter Symi Square through the Liberation Gate (Pyli Eleftherias). This gate was opened by the Italians in 1924 in the belief that it was they who had liberated Rhodes from the Turkish occupation. Exactly opposite are the ruins of a **Temple of Aphrodite** from the 3rd century B.C. Behind this temple is the inn of the **Langue of Auvergne** built in 1507. This inn now houses governmental offices. To the Left, the Arsenal Gate leads to the commercial harbor. Symi Square was also called Arsenal Square because it was believed this is where the Knights had their naval station or arsenal. The building to the right has the Ionian Bank on the ground floor and the **Municipal Gallery** on the upper floor. Its collection also contains the work of modern Greek painters.

From here the street goes slightly uphill to Argyrokastro Square which is small and picturesque with a beautiful fountain in the middle. Argyrokastro Square contains one of the oldest buildings around the Castle area which today houses the **Historical** and **Archaeological Institute**. To the left of the Archaeological Institute is the **Folklore Museum**. Continuing along you pass under an arch and come out before the Cathedral Church of the Knights, the **Church of Our Lady of the Castle** which is at the beginning of the Knights' Street. The original church was probably Byzantine, built in the 12th century. Immediately after the church Our Lady of the Castle is Museum Square where the Inn of the Langue of England is and the Knights' hospital.

Argyrokastro Square with an Early Christian Bapistry in the middle.

Symi Square. The Municipal Gallery is above the Ionian Bank.

The Archaeological Museum
(Knghts' Hospital)

To your right as you advance toward the square is the **Knights' Hospital**. It is in nearly perfect condition and underlines the original purpose of the Order, which was to house and treat suffering pilgrims from the Holy Lands and later the Crusaders. Now it houses the **Archaeological Museum** of Rhodes. Large and imposing, it is perhaps the most important building of the Knights in the town.

It began to be built in 1440 by the Grand Master de Lastic and was completed in 1484 by the Grand Master Pierre d'Aubusson. On the ground floor, right and left of the entrance, are arched openings to the storerooms, now used as commercial shops. Near the middle of the building, the main entrance is through a similar opening, framed with carved decoration. Directly above this entrance is a three-sided niche with windows "breaking" the monolithic and practically bare facade of the upper floor. This three-sided niche is a part of the chapel in the great hall on the upper floor. The main entrance leads through a colonnade into the inner courtyard which is surrounded on all four sides by a two-storey arcade with low-arched openings. The upper floor is reached by a magnificent staircase in the NE corner of the courtyard.

Right: The entrance to the Archaeological Museum which is of great interest not only for its exhibits but for the building itself.

Below: its interior courtyard.

The Street of the Knights

Returning to Museum Square you enter the **Street of the Knights**. This was the main street in the Collachium and is perhaps the best preserved medieval street one will find in Europe, the only one that has retained its authentic character. During the early years of the Turkish occupation the buildings were used as barracks. The earlier shape of the street was later restored by Italian archaeologists. It has a length of about 200 m. and a width of 6 m. and goes uphill toward the Palace of the Grand Masters. Right and left of it are the inns of the various nationalities, the Langues that we have mentioned.

As you enter the Street of the Knights, to your left is the north facade of the Hospital (Museum). This is directly followed by the Inn of the Langue of Italy.

Next to it is a **small palace** whose facade bears the coats-of-arms of the French Grand Masters Aimerie d'Amboise and Philip Villiers de l'Isle Adam. Opposite this palace was the original main entrance to the Hospital. Immediately after it, behind an iron gate is a deeply-shaded garden with a Turkish fountain.

Practically opposite the garden, is the Inn of the **Langue of France** the most lavishly decorated of all the inns and one of the most beautiful of the Knights' buildings. Next to the Inn is the Chapel of the Langue of France along with a Gothic statue of the Virgin Mary and Child on its facade. The coat-of-arms of the Grand Master Raymond Beranger (from 1365 to 1374) is on the chapel showing that it was built during his time and consequently is one of the oldest buildings on the Knights' Street. The chapel is right next to the residence of the priest of the Langue of France which now houses the Italian Consulate. These three impressive French buildings show the dominant position of the French in the Order.

The statue of Virgin and Child, on the facade of the Langue of France.

Right after this an arch with a room above it cuts through the Knights' Street at right angles. As soon as you pass the arch and to your right is the Inn of the **Langue of Provence** and on your left the Inn of the **Langue of Spain**. A little beyond these last two inns on the Street of the Knights, a large, restored Gothic loggia brings the street to a monumental end. This loggia, built in the first half of the 15th century, connected the Palace of the Grand Masters with the church of Saint John, which was built in the first half of the 14th century and was the official church of the Order. In 1865 a bolt of lighting ignited a large quantity of gunpowder which lay forgotten in its cellars. The explosion blew the church to bits, destroyed the neighboring loggia and whatever still remained from the abandoned palace of the Grand Masters. But the design of the church still survived in Rottiers' drawings and based on them the Italians built a church with the same name at Mandraki, near the Law Courts, now called the Church of the Annunciation (Evangelismos).

The Knights street, a classical example of the coexistence of the past and the present in Rhodes.

The Palace of the Grand Masters

Opposite the Church of Saint John, at the highest point of the Castle, stands **The Palace of the Grand Masters** which was the administrative center and the Knights' "Acropolis". It had very imposing dimensions (80x75 m.) and defensive fortifications. It was so strong that during the siege of 1522 it suffered little damage.

On the site where the palace stands (Castello) the "Lower Acropolis" of ancient Rhodes once stood. This is also where the acropolis of the Rhodians of the Byzantine period stood (7th century). The arrangement of the palace around the central courtyard with the apartments on the first floor and the storerooms on the ground floor show the Byzantine influences at work.

During the early years of their occupation, the Turks used it as a prison and then left it to crumble. The palace was completely destroyed by the great explosion at the church of St. John in 1865.

The Italians rebuilt it on the ruins of the old one, as faithfully as possible, and completed it in 1940. Its floors are decorated with marvelous mosaics of the Hellenistic and Roman period which were brought in from Kos (see page 67). The statues in the inner courtyard of the palace are also from the Hellenistic and Roman period. There are indications that under its foundations lies the famous ancient temple of Helios with its lavish decoration.

Panoramic view of the palace and impressive entrance.

Leaving the palace, you see Cleovulou Square on your right. Just beyond this square you enter a wonderful wide street shaded by plane trees. This is Orpheos Street. To your right, on a wall which connects the interior wall of Castello with the exterior, is the Gate of St. Anthony and the, turning left, the majestic Amboise Gate. Between these two gates you will have the chance to sit down and rest on iron benches under the plane trees and, why not, pose for a quick portrait by one of the artists who hang out there.

Turning back in the other direction along Orpheos Street you will see, on the left, the Clock Tower (built after the earthquake of 1851) on the site where the southwest medieval tower of the inner wall of Castello once stood.

Between St. Anthonios Gate and d'Amboise Gate (foto1), the Orpheos St.(foto 3,4) artists sit under the plane trees. The clock tower (built after the earthquake of 1851) (foto 2).

Chora or Bourgo

Just outside the inner wall of the Collachium you arrive at the **long bazaar** at the top of Sokratous St. To your left is the **Mosque of Suleiman**, situated in a beautiful courtyard with plane trees. It was built in 1808 on the site of an older one which had been built in honor of Suleiman the Magnificent, the conqueror of Rhodes. On the opposite side of the street is the **Turkish Library Achmed Hafouz** which was founded in 1794 by this Moslem man from Rhodes.

Apollonion St. sets off from near the mosque of Suleiman and heads toward the west side of the walls. Here one finds the Byzantine Gothic church of Ayios Georgios (St. George). This elegant church from the 15th century was used by the Turks as a Theological School.

Turning back, the first street on the right (Ippodamou St.) takes you to the old Turkish quarter which has lost practically nothing of its medieval flavor. On the right side of the street you will see the Church of Ayia Paraskevi from the 15th century built in a free cruciform shape. The first street after Ayia Paraskevi (Archelaou St.) leads to Arionos Square where the **Sultan Mustapha Mosque** stands; it was built in 1765 and is followed by the Turkish baths.

A lane heads down from Arionos square to the outdoor **Theater of the Old Town** where folk dance companies perform every evening during summer. The street ends at Ayiou Fanouriou St. You turn right and come upon the small Byzantine church of Ayios Fanourios which the Turks made into a mosque. Some marvelous wall paintings have been preserved under the plaster the Turks put over on the interior walls.

5

6

5.6. Sokratous St. the "long bazaar"
    with an endless variety of souvenirs.

View of the medieval town.

The Ippokratos Square with a view of the medieval buildings of "Castellania".

Returning to Ayiou Fanouriou St. and following it to the north, you will come to Sokratous St., the bustling street of the bazaar with its endless variety of souvenirs.

Heading down toward the harbor you enter Ippokratous Square with a beautiful Turkish fountain in its center. Here is part of an important building of the Knights knows as "**Castellania**" with a large external staircase. It was built in 1597 and was an important commercial center. On the ground floor the merchants carried out their exchanges while the upper floor was used as a courtroom to settle their disputes. On the south side of Ippokratous Square, Pythagora St. leads to the Mosque of **Imbrahim Pasha**. A few meters beyond the square is the Marine Gate, framed by two towers making it perhaps the most spectacular gate in the Castle. As can be seen from copperplates from the last century, the sea came right up to it.

From Ippokratous Square, Aristotelous St. leads to the old Jewish quarter and to the Square of Jewish Martyrs, where there is a charming little fountain decorated with shells, starfish, octopi and the like set on blue tiles with three large metal seahorses in the background.

On the north side of the square is a noteworthy building from the 15th century, the **Palace of the Admirals**. Before the Turkish occupation it housed the Orthodox Archbishop of Rhodes.

Continuing along Pindarou St. (an extension of Aristotelous) you will come on the ruins of the Gothic church of **Our Lady of Chora** (Sainte Marie de Bourg) which was the largest Catholic church in Rhodes (30X18 m.). A part of the church lies on the left side of the street and the other on the right.

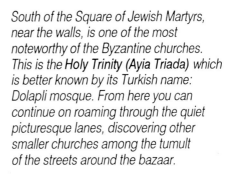

South of the Square of Jewish Martyrs, near the walls, is one of the most noteworthy of the Byzantine churches. This is the **Holy Trinity (Ayia Triada)** which is better known by its Turkish name: Dolapli mosque. From here you can continue on roaming through the quiet picturesque lanes, discovering other smaller churches among the tumult of the streets around the bazaar.

1. The ruins of the Church of Our Lady of Chora, right and left of the street.

2. The Byzantine Church of the Holy Trinity south of the Square of Jewish Martyrs.

3. The fountain in the center of the Square of Jewish Martyrs.

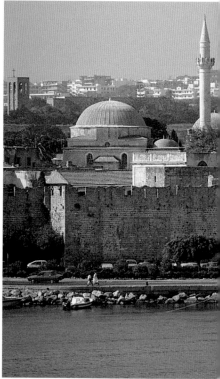

The Walls of the Castle

The main contribution that the first Knights to arrive made to the fortification of the town, were the repairs to the old Byzantine walls. These major works which gave the walls their final form were carried out by the Grand Master d'Aubusson, particularly after the failure of the Turkish siege of 1480. During this period the round towers appeared and became dominant because they were able to deflect cannon balls, unlike the square towers which were much more vulnerable. The thickness of the walls was raised to 12 meters and the moat made more than 21 meters wide.

The walls (approximately four kilometers long) were divided into sections and each section was guarded by one of the Order's "Langues".

The walls of the Castle constitute an interesting example of military architecture which reflects a period of transition during which the use of cannons brought about great changes in defenses when the former fortification works showed how powerless they were against the power of gunpowder.

Above right: the impressive Marine gate (Porta Marina).
Below: The Arsenal Gate (Tarsana) on the NW end of the harbor.

6

MUSEUMS

Archaeological - Folklore -
The Municipal Gallery - Castello

The Archaeological Museum

The Archaeological Museum lies in the middle of the medieval town (see page 64). The museum contains a significant number of sculptures and other works of art.

Among the most noteworthy exhibits are the following:

– Two archaic **Kouroi** which were found at Kameiros. Both of these statues are from the 6th century and were made nearly at the same time. Even though both of them reveal a large Egyptian influence the more recent one shows that the sculptor had a better knowledge of anatomy and the movement of the human body.

– A marble **head of the god Helios** from the 2nd century B.C. was found behind the Inn of the

The marble lion in the courtyrad of the museum. It stanbds opposite the main entrance to the Knights' Hospital which has housed the Archaeological Museum of Rhodes since 1916.

Langue of Pro-vence, that is, near the top of Castello where the ancient temple of the god Helios is said to have been. The thick hair of the god is ringed with holes to which metal "sun rays" must have been fitted.

– Two lovely statues of Aphrodite. The first is called the Thalassia ("Marine") Aphrodite because it was found in the sea on the western coast of the island. It is from the 4th century B.C. and is larger than lifesize. The goddess is depicted as half-nude with a garment that reaches down to her waist. The other depicts Aphrodite nude and is known as the Aphrodite of Rhodes. The goddess is kneeling having just emerged from the sea and is wringing the water from her hair. The statue, 49 cm. high, is dated to the 1st century B.C. and is made of Parian marble.

The marble statue of the Aphrodite of Rhodes, in a room of the Archaeological Museum that was named after it.

— The famous marble funerary stele of **Crito and Timarista** which is also from the necropolis at Kameiros. It is dated to the end of the 5th century B.C. and depicts two women, a mother and her daughter. The mother, Timarista, is embracing her daughter Crito before they part forever. Crito with her hair cut short as a sign of mourning, is stroking her mother's shoulder while Timarista's right leg and arm appear to being lightly moving outside the frame and outside the world itself.

The museum also has valuable finds from the cemeteries of Ialyssos and Kameiros on display: pots, jewellery, scarabs and Rhodian amphorae. There is a lavish collection of coins from antiquity and the time of the Knights as well as early Christian inscriptions, coats-of-arms from the tombstones of the Knights and so on.

1. *Funerary stele of Crito and Timarista (5th century B.C.).*

2. *Statue of Zeus from Kameiros from Hellenistic times. (Hall of the small Aphrodite).*

3. *A large hall with marble tombstones done in relief from the time of the Knights.*

Funerary steele of Calliarista (4th century B.C.)

A typical Rhodian vase in the "Fikelloura" style with a number of partridges (6th century B.C.).

The courtyrad of Archaeological Museum.

Castello

The Palace of the Grand Masters dominates the medieval town. The large entrance is located on the south side of the palace. There are three decorated rooms with wall paintings by the painter Vellana, done 1940; they are just after the covered space on the right. Marble statues that were found in the ancient Odeion of Kos have been placed on the north side of the inner courtyard.

The corridor that passes in front of the chapel leads to the exhibition space on the ground floor.

The first floor of the palace is impressive for its luxury and its wealth. It consists of many rooms decorated with relief depictions, mosaic floors, statues, vases, furniture and portable icons.

The Folklore Museum

The museum is housed in a building from the time of the Knights which occupies nearly all the south side of Argyrokastrou Square. The marvellously preserved collection on display includes furniture, ceramics, handiwork, traditional costumes and other items of traditional Dodecanesian art.

The Municipal gallery

It is located in Symi Square in the medieval town. Its collections include the works of modern Greek painters.

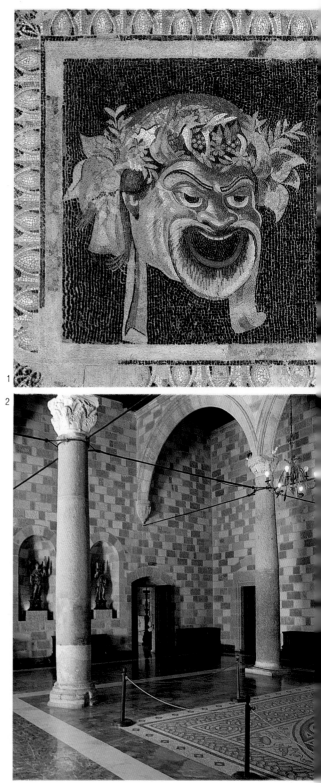

1. Theatrical mask, a mosaic from Hellenistic times.

2. The room of colonnades. One of the rooms one can visit in the palace with its mosaic floor, carved wooden furniture and angelic-looking candlesticks. On the left page, below: the interior courtyard

3. The seahorse and the nymph (a mosaic floor from the room of the palace with the same name from the 1st century B.C.).

4. The interior courtyard of Castello.

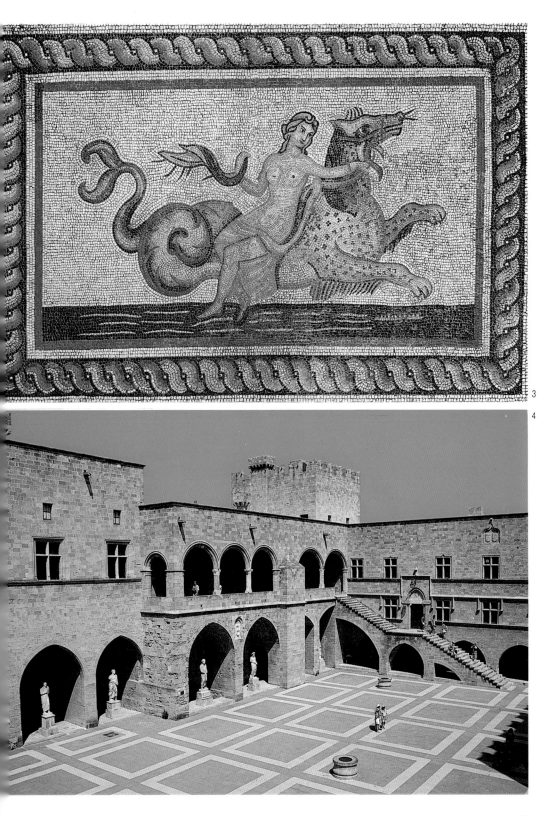

7

THE TOWN OF RHODES

The Ancient Town - The Modern Town
Rhodini Park - Mount Smith

The ships from Piraeus usually arrive at Rhodes at dawn. At that time the sun gilding the sea also gilds the two statues -- a stag and a doe -- that have been set up on the columns at the entrance to the ancient harbor and together constitute the island's symbol. Tradition has it the famous Colossus, one of the seven wonders of the ancient world, stood on the same site. It was an enormous bronze statue which depicted the god Helios holding a flaming torch. One of his legs stood on one side of the harbor and the other on the other and the ships passed between them. This is one of the loveliest towns in the whole Mediterranean, built at the northernmost point of the island. The sea surrounds it and a gleaming sun lights it for almost the entire year. It combines the cosmopolitan character of a completely modern town with the picturesqueness of the old medieval town which seems untouched by the passage of time. Opposite the statues of the stag and the doe and a little above the old harbor

The entrance to Mandraki.

is the commanding Castello, the Palace of the Grand Masters of the Knights of Rhodes. Next to it lies the medieval town (see Medieval town). The town of Rhodes, with its 41,000 inhabitants, lies on the same site where in 408 B.C. ancient Rhodes was built. Its life has gone on uninterrupted for 2,400 years leaving monu-ments from all the historical periods, the one right next to the other. Present-day Rhodes has an impressive variety of colors and shapes: captivating beaches, modern buildings, picturesque neighborhoods, imposing medieval edifices, Byzantine churches and minarets. The greenery in the town is something unique. There is riotous vegetation around the walls of the medieval castle; all the palm trees give it a tropical flavor. There are hotels, restaurants, tavernas and the night clubs for entertainment as well as the commercial shops number in the hundreds. From April to October the town is transformed into an international center where the foreigners outnumber the locals.

The Ancient Town

To the east of the new town is an important piece of ancient Rhodes. It is the ancient harbor, the present-day Mandraki, with the statues of the stag and the doe at its entrance. The ancient town of Rhodes was founded in 408 B.C. with the three largest towns on the island (Lindos, Ialyssos and Kameiros) joining together to create it; this was at the initiative of Dorieas, the son of the Olympic victor Diagoras. The new capital was a landmark in the history of the island, and was also called Rhodes; it was located in the same position as the present one.

Lucian called Rhodes the "true daughter of the Sun" and added that it it had the same beauty "Helios" did. The much-travelled Strabo wrote that "Rhodes is so different from the rest of the places that I cannot compare it to any of them". Finally, Horace, in admiring it, called it "glorious Rhodes".

The temples in the town that are outstanding for their brilliance and their wealth are those dedicated to the god Helios, and to Asclepius, Zeus Savior, Hera and Dionysios. The latter was decorated with inimitable works of sculpture and painting, true masterpieces done by local and foreign artists. The temple of Helios was renowned because that is where the quadriga chariot of the god was found, one of the most beautiful creations of Lysippos. A similar chariot was dedicated by the Rhodians to Delphi. The horses of the Delphic group are the ones people today admire at St.

Mandraki, the harbor of ancient Rhodes with the statues of the stag and the doe at its entrance.

It was built on a plan laid out according to the "Hippodamian System", that is, based on a system of main streets which went from east to west and from north to south.

These roads met at junctions thus forming square corners.

From the descriptions of ancient writers and the inferences drawn from excavations we can conclude that Rhodes was one of the loveliest towns in the ancient world.

"The most beautiful of Greek towns no matter where" as the Sophist Ailios Aristeidis deemed it with admiration, describing the harbor and the moles, the shipyards (where the Rhodians built their renowned ships), the temples, the numerous civic buildings, the gymnasiums, the racetracks and so on.

Mark's in Venice. But statues were not only used to decorate the temples and other places of worship; they were also used on the streets and the civic edifices as well. Cassius transported nearly thee thousand sculptures to Rome with which he decorated the temples, palaces and the public spaces of the "Eternal City".

It was also impressive the way the buildings were constructed in ancient Rhodes being so alike it was as if the entire town was one extended house. Finally, the walls that surrounded the town for a distance of approximately 15 kilometers made with their lofty towers such a sight that the Sophist Aristeides wrote "the eyes of man never tires of gazing a them".

Of the superb works in the town little has been left for the visitor to admire because of time, the terrible earthquakes, the invasions and other disasters. But these few things are enough to give one a picture of a magnificent civilization and bear witness to the beauty and the grandeur that was lost. To the south its walls reach up to the hills which rise above them and separate the northern level triangle from the rest of the island (Mount Smith hill).

The area inside the walls is calculated to be around 70 hectares. The population of the ancient town in the 3rd and the 2nd century B.C. is thought to have been around 80,000. There were two acropolises in the environs of the walls: the one on Mount Smith hill and the other, smaller one, where the Knights' Castello is located today. When in 1522 the Turks pillaged the town of Castle, they settled there and left only the Jews in the neighborhood where they had been. The Greeks were forced out of the town and they were permitted to live only in neighborhoods outside the walls, known by the name **"Marasia"**. These neighborhoods were created south and southeast of the Castle where during the time of the Knights there had been country houses and churches. The new neighborhoods took their names from these churches. During the past hundred years or so a new quarter has been created called Niochori ("New Town"), on the north coast, where all those who come from the surrounding islands reside as well as other outsiders, mainly Europeans. Here is where the Italians built the new buildings that form the center of the town. The town has now expanded, with new neighborhoods, to Mount Smith hill and to the other hills further south.

THE NEW & MEDIEVAL TOWN OF RHODES

Legend for the New Town

1. Kyprou Square
2. New Market
3. RODA Buses
4. KTEL Buses
5. Entrance to Mandraki
6. Medieval Windmills
7. Ayios Nikolaos Fortress
8. Bank of Greece
9. Law Courts
10. Post Office
11. Evangelismos Church.
12. Prefecture (Governer's Palace)
13. Town Hall
14. National Theater
15. Murat Reis Mosque

16. Naval Society
17. Acquarium
18. Tennis Court
19. Casino
20. Offices of Olympic Airways
21. Phone Company (OTE)
22. National Tourist Organization
23. Taxi Stand
24. Hospital

Mount Smith

25. Ancient Theater
26. Ancient Stadium
27. Temple of Apollo
28. Diagoras Stadium

Getting to know the New Town

You set off on your tour of the New Town from Kyprou Square, the heart of its most lavish market. There you will find some of the finest boutiques in Rhodes, jewellery stores, fabric shops and tailor shops and nearly all the banks. Heading down Gallias Street you will encounter a large, heptagonal building, the **New Market**. Dozens of shops on the ground floor and offices on the upper floor enclose a large space where there are green-grocers, butchers, fishmongers and snack-bars and cafeterias. From here you will see a part of the Palace of the Grand Masters and in the most beautiful of gardens the presentations of **Sound and Light**. Continuing on another 100 meters from the New market you will reach **Mandraki harbour**. It was the military harbor of ancient Rhodes whose entrance was sealed off by chains. The long breakwater at Mandraki holds the three medieval **windmills** which ground the wheat unloaded by the merchant ships. From here can be seen the large commercial harbor of Rhodes, Emborio as it is called and, a little to the south, the secondary harbor of Akandia. At the end of the breakwater the **Fortress of Ayios Nikolaos** commands the harbour. It was built in the 15th century by the Knights of Rhodes to strengthen their defenses against Turkish attacks.

1. *Kyprou Square.*
2. *The entrance to the new market in front of Mandraki harbor with Castello to the rear.*
3. *The Mandraki breakwater and the medieval windmills and the St. Nikolas fortress to the rear.*
4. *The garden where the "Sound and Light" shows are held.*

1

2

3

4

From the coastal avenue (Eleftheras Square), which runs parallel with the mole on the harbor, there are urban buses that come and go every half hour doing their run through the town. Following the avenue north you pass successively past the **Bank of Greece**, **The Law Courts** and the **Post Office**. Opposite the Post Office is the **Church of the Evangelismos (Annunciation)** which was built like the Knight's church of St. John which then lay opposite the Palace of the Grand Masters. It is the town's Cathedral Church. A little further on is the **Governor's Mansion (Prefecture)**, which lies exactly opposite the **Town Hall** and the **National Theater**. All the above buildings were built during the Italian occupation (1912-1943). Next to the National Theater is the small but noteworthy **Mosque of Murat Reis**, with an elegant white minaret. Here you will find the old Muslim cemetery.

To the north, exactly opposite the entrance to the harbor, is the **Naval Society** where young men and women are trained in sailing, rowing and swimming. A very lovely sandy beach starts at the Naval Society and extends to the northernmost point of the island where the **Acquarium** is. The sandy beach also extends to the southwest. Every summer thousands of tourists dedicate themselves to the worship of the sun, something which is in accord with the island's mythology since the Sun God (Helios) held a special place in the pantheon of the ancient Rhodians.

1. The church of Annunciation (Evangelismos).

2. Liberation Square.

3. The National Theater.

4. The Street of Date-Palms.

5. The Governor' Palace (Prefecture).

6. The Acquarium
   and the sand beach on the north side of the town.

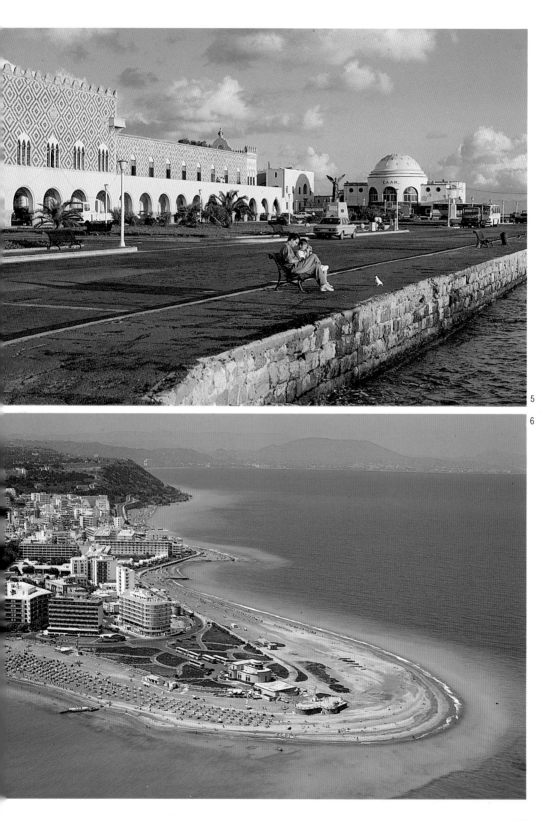

Rhodini Park

The park is about 3 km. from the center of the town along the road that goes to Lindos.
Rhodini Park is a verdant deeply-shaded ravine with running water and ponds with water-lilies. Within this ideal environment peacocks live and breed giving the place its own, exotic color.
It is has been maintained that Rhodini is where the ancient School of Rhetoric was.
If you walk for about ten minutes beside the river bed you will find a tomb that was cut out of the rock; it is mistakenly known as the Tomb of the Ptolemies. The rock has been removed in such a way as to form the large square base of a grave each side measuring 27.80 m.
Each side is also decorated with 21 Doric half-columns. It is from the Hellenistic period and was restored in 1924.

Mount Smith Hill
(The Upper Acropolis of Ancient Rhodes)

One can go on foot (it is less than 3 km. from the center of the town) or by urban bus.

The hill took its name from the English admiral Sir Sydney Smith who had his observation post here in 1802 to keep an eye on the movements of Napoleon's fleet during his war with the Turks.

Just south of the top of the hill are a group of important ancient monuments. In a natural hollow lies the **Stadium**, a work most probably of the 2nd century B.C. which has in large part been rebuilt. It is 200 m. long and 35 m. wide. Here well-known Greek and foreign groups give concerts during the summer. Next to the Stadium is a small Theater whose reconstruction in white marble was made possible by the few remaining ancient ruins. It has been conjectured it was used for the classes of the famed School of Rhetoric rather than for theatrical performances.

A bit further up, the area is commanded by the large **Temple of Pythian Apollo**. From the few remains a corner of the temple was reconstructed. The three above buildings along with the fabulous **Gymnasium** constituted one of the man focuses of artistic life on ancient Rhodes.

*General view
of the archaeological site of Mount Smith.*

The upper acropolis of ancient Rhodes was on top of the hill. The lower acropolis was on the site where the Castello of the medieval town was erected.
The view from here is magnificent, both toward the island and toward the sea, the nearby islands and the coast of Asia Minor. But you are advised to go in the afternoon in order to enjoy, along with everything else, the dark red sun as it slowly dips below the horizon.
Above, left: the renovated theater.

1. The archaeological site of Mount Smith to the rear of the bay of Ialyssos.

2. The renovated theater.

3. View of the archaeological site with a glimpse of the northeastern side of the island.

4. The temple of Pythian Apollo on the top of a hill with a view of the Medieval Town.

8

THE EAST COAST

Koskinou - Kallithea - Faliraki - Afantou
Kolybia - Archangelos - Kattavia - Prasonisi

On this excursion you will get to know the entire east coast of Rhodes, setting off from the town and going to the southernmost tip of the island, Prasonisi. This excursion covers 102 km. and world-famous Lindos, the Aegean village at the foot of a hill, with its imposing ancient acropolis, is about at the half-way point of the excursion. But besides that the east coast is veritable wonderland for the visitor starting with the touristically developed areas that extend from the town of Rhodes to Lindos and ending at the beautiful and unspoiled Prasonisi, which is joined to the rest of the island Rhodes by a strip of sand. You can do this entire excursion in one day, stopping for a few hours in Lindos, for a pleasant swim in one of its picturesque coves and then have a meal in a small taverna or, if you prefer, swim at one of the more cosmopolitan beaches which have dozens of restaurants. On this excursion you will have the chance to go through Kallithea, with its lovely old spas, and then Faliraki with its beaches of golden sand and up-to-date hotel complexes; this is followed by Kolymbia, the popular beach of Tsambika, the traditional village of Archangelos, the village of Lardas nestled in greenery, the fishing settlement of Kiotari, the village of Gennadi until at last you reach the southernmost village in Rhodes, Kattavia, where there is a road that takes you to Prasonisi. The variety of the natural landscape combined with the many exceptional sites spurs the visitor to explore on his own. The entire excursion is filled with archaeological sites, castles, monasteries, villages with a strong folk character, mountains and springs as well as one sandy beach after the other and picturesque leeward coves suitable to varied tastes and all this on a very short excursion. So get the things you need and go off and hav a gret time!

Koskinou-Kallithea

You will take the coastal road leading out of
Rhodes and reach Faliraki after passing
through the seaside settlement of Ayia Marina.
You will reach Reni beach outside the village of
Koskinou. The rocky coast hides many
gorgeous little coves and sand beaches. Some
of the largest and best hotel comoplexes on
the island have been built above these coves.
The beach is less than 500 m. from the main
road. A turn-off to the right leads after 2 km. to
the village of **Koskinou**. The village itself lies
eight km. from the town of Rhodes and is in the
middle of an area of fruit-trees. It has a good
road network and is served by the national
road from Rhodes to Lindos as well as by the
provincial Rhodes - Kallithea - Faliraki road.
The village of Koskinou has been declared
subject to preservation because of its unique and
lovely traditional houses which are visited by
thousands of summer vacationers every year.
They are ornamented with multicolred cermaic
plates and weaving while their flower-filled
courtyards are paved with blak-and-white pebbles.
There is a major festival on the name-day of
the St. Marina (Ayia Marina) on July 17.
Tourism Day is celebrated locally on
September 27 with the customary music,
dancing and singing. The area is also noted for
the church of Ayios Loukas (St. Luke) from the
4th century and Ayia Eirene (St. Eirene, 19th
century) located in the village.
Continuing along the coast road you reach the
town of **Kallithea** 11 k., further on. Its springs
with their medicinal waters, which used to
attract many people suddering from various
ailments, are no longer in operation but it is
worth having a look at the spas themselves
and having a swim in onr the quiet little bays.
The renovation and reopening of the springs is
now being planned.

1. Traditional houses in Koskinou.
2. The gorgeous coves along the cosmopolitan
   coast of Koskinou.
3. The picturesque little harbor of Kallithea.
4. The courtyards are paved with blak-and-white pebbles.

Faliraki

*From Kallithea the road goes uphill
to the south and one km. later you
see the famous beach of **Faliraki**
spreading out before you, over 5 km.
of golden sand and crystal-clear
sea. Ultramodern hotel units have
been built along this coast which
can satisfy all your requirements.
You can also enjoy a full range of
marine sports. There are
competitions throughout the
celebration of Naval Week.
You can also get to Faliraki on the
main road from Rhodes to Lindos
(16 km.).*

*Above: The church of Ayios Nektarios
to Faliraki and the beautiful beach
with its modern hotel units at Faliraki.*

Kalythies

*To the right of Faliraki is the village of **Kalythies** with its narrow lanes, spic-and-span and the church of Timios Stavros which has its major celebration on September 14. You can also see the iconostasis of the church of the Transfiguration of christ from the 16th century. The surroundings are a mixture of monuments and picturesque landscapes. Olive groves on the plains, pine trees and antiquities on the mountains. The **Eleousa Monastery**, north of the village, has marvelous wall paintings and two coats-of-arms from the period of the Knights. The Acropolis of **Sarandapichos**, the oldest one in northern Rhodes, lies to the west as one goes toward the village of Maritsa. The cave of Ayios Georgios (St. George) on one side of Psinthos has stalactites and is generally considered to be the oldest Neolithic settlement on the island.*

Ladiko

*After Faliraki you can turn left and go to the peaceful and deep blue waters of the small bay of Ladiko, one of the most picturesque inlets in all of Rhodes. The **Erimokastro** fortress lies on the elevation between **Ladiko** and the bay of Afantou. The entrance to the acropolis and parts of three of the towers can be seen. Tombs extending from the Mycenean to the Roman period were found below the fortress. There is an impressive view toward the beach at Afantou and Ladiko. The main road goes on and to the left is the monastery of **Profitis Amos** (Prophet Amos) with wall paintings from the 18th century.*
The single aisled basilica has wall paintings from the 18th century and celebrates on 15 June.

The deep blue bay of Ladiko.

Afantou

If you take the road from Rhodes to Lindos, 5 km. after Faliraki you will come to the village of Afantou, on your right, while **Afantou** beach is on your left. The village of Afantou, surrounded by fruit-trees and olive groves, is one of the largest and oldest villageas on Rhodes with roots deeply embedded in the history and tradition of the island and is pariculrly adept at carpet-weaving. There is the commanding Church of the Panayia (Virgin Mary) next to the main square. Along the road to the beach is the Panayia tis Catholikis (The Catholic Virgin Mary) with wall paintigs from the 17th century which celebrates its name day on August 15th. The extensive beach at Afantou has clean water and small pebbles. The golf course of Rhodes is nearby.

The traditional village of Afantou with its extensive beach.

Kolybia

4 km. past Afantou you will reach the picturesque village of **Kolybia**.
A road shaded by towering eucalyptus trees leads from the village to the seaside, where there are wonderful sandy inlets. The tourist resort of Kolybia offers one beautiful beaches and modern hotel units so that the visitor can have a comfortable and pleasant stay. This is also an ideal area for fishing.

1. *The road lined with eucalpytus trees which leads to the coast at Kolymbia.*

2. *Kolymbia, with its marvellous sandy coves and up-to-the-minute hotel units.*

Kolybia - Epta Piges

At Kolybia you can turn right and head inland and 3.5 km. later you will reach **Epta Piges** (Seven Springs). This is a beautiful deep green ravine with plane trees with gushing water both winter and summer, forming small streams. All of this water is collected in an artificial lake and then is used to irrigate the plain of Kolybia. One reaches the artifical lake by going through the same channel the water goes through. The road goes west from here to the islandYs interior and there are many turn-ofs to be explored.

Tsabika

Three km. after Kolybia you turn left and go past a hill which has the Tsabika monastery at its summit and then you go to the lovely, popular beach of the same name which is 1.5 km. from the main road. It is a beach of golden snd and its clean refreshing water makes it ideal for swimming and marine sports. It is even better to go to **Tsabika beach** on a caique, which makes for a pleasant day cruise. Before the turn-off that leads to the beach there is a turn-off to the left that goes to the monastery of the **Panayia tis Tsabika e Kyra** (The Virgin Mary of Tsabika, or Our Blessed Lady) on the top of a verdant hill. The road goes 3/4 of the way uo. It takes 15 minutes more to walk to the top (height 287 meters) from where you can enjoy a panoramic view of the beaches of Afantou, Kolybia and Tabika and the interior of the island (all the way to Mt. Attavyros). The monastery was built in the 16th century. Its feast-day is on September 8 and there is a traditional frestival. The church has breath-taking interior decoration and a miracle-working icon of the Annunciation.

3. The lovely dark green ravine of Epta Piges.

4. The coast at Tsabika, with its golden sand and crytsal-clear water an idea place for swimming and marine sports.

The large, traditional village of Archangelos and Stegna beach, just to the east of it.

Archangelos - Stegna - Charaki

Four km. after Tsabika, going up the road from Rhodes to Lindos, you reach the village of **Archangelos**. *It is a traditional village, the main one in th area with small carpet-making and cermaic industries. Though it has all the tourist comforts Archangelos still retains its traditional color. There are musical and dancing events during its Cultural Week held from the 12 to 20 August. On the top of a hill near the village are the ruins of a medieval castle which was built by the Grand Master Orsini in 1467.*

Just before Archangelos a road goes down for 2 km. to the beach of **Stegna**. *The bay has its own special beauty and is rimmed with greenery. On the main road outside the village is the* **Monastery of Ayioi Theodoroi** *(Saint Theodore) with wall paintings from the 14th century.*

Four km. after Archangelos a turn-off left leads to **Charaki** *after 3 km. This is the coastal resort settlement connected to the villages of Malonas and Masari with a view of Lindos.*

Feraklos Castle

One km. before Charaki a turn-off to the left leads after 800 m. to an incredibly lovely cove with a beach of fine gold sand. Between this small bay and Charaki is the medieval **Feraklos** *Castle perched on the top of a hill. It was one of the last fortifications to fall to the Turks. The Knights used it as a detention center for captives and for other Knights who had transgressed the rules of the Order. From Archangelos you can go along the old road that passes through the villages of Malonas and Masari. This side-trip goes through the fertile falley of Naithonas, covered with orange groves. Northwest of the the village of Malonas is the* **Monastery of Stavros** *(The Monastery of the Cross). The village of Masari combines the comaraderie of its unaffected inhabitants with the enjoyment all its greenery affords. The picturesque* **Kamyri Monastery** *lies between the two villages in the midst of a thick woods; its is over a thousand years old and is dedicated to the Archangel Michael.*

The coast at Charaki with the medieval castle of Feraklos in the background.

Kalathos - Vlycha - Lindos

Staying on the road to Lindos you will reach the village of Kalathos 7 km. after the village of Masari. This was the ancient deme ("commons") of Lindos, Klasioi. After Kalathos the road heads straight on to Lindos while if you turn to the right you will go to the southern villages of Rhodes and going left you will go down to the stunnning bay of **Vlycha** with its enormous sand beach. This was the grazing and farmland of Lindos during the period when the Knights ruled the island. Near the beach is the Church of the Blessed Virgin of Eulo, cut out of the rock; it has wall paintings from the 14th century. The acropolis of Lindos makes its majestic appearance just after one passes Vlycha bay.

Lindos is an Aegean village and together with its imposing acropolis offers one a unique and unforgetable experience. You return to the main road whch is above Vlycha bay. The road passes through a valley which is the main way of getting to the interior and southern villages of the island.

Beautiful Vlycha bay just outside Lindos.

Lardos - Ypsenis Monastery - Pefkoi

The village of **Pylonas** is found in this valley along with the Evagelismos Church with wall paintings from the 14th century. Tombs from the Minoan period were found in the are of Aspropylia. Six km. from the turn-off is the village of Lardos nestled deep in a green landscape. A road winding through 5 km. of wooded mountains leads to the **Monastery of Panayia Ypseni** which has an iconostasis made of olive wood. Two km. from the village is the gorgeous beach of Lardos with its clear and deep blue water and its fabulous shores. The resort settlement of **Pefkoi** lies on the east side of the bay. A turn-off from Lardos leads, after 12 km., to the village of Laerma in the center of the island. The road continues on to the southern villages passing by deserted beaches and wonderful little bays.

1. *The church of the Archangel Michael in the village of Lardos.*
2. *The resort settlement of Pefkoi.*
3. *The bay of Lardos.*

Kiotari - Asklepieio

The resort settlement of **Kiotari** lies nine km. from Lardos. Kiotari is to the north of the huge bay of Gennadi and has very clean water and a pebbled beach. Its natural harbor is made use of by all kinds of amateur fishermen.

Four km. northwest of Kiotari is the traditional Aegean settlement of **Asklepieio** built on the side of a hill with small, dazzlingly white houses and narrow lanes. At the entrance to the village is the Byzantine church of the Dormition of the Virgin. It has wall paintings, was built in the 11th century and celebrates its name-day on August 15. There is an ecclesiastical and folklore museum in the town. The hill is dominated by a Byzantine Venetian fotress from 1200. Next to the resort settlement of Kiotari is the small monastery of The **Metamorphosis tou Sotiros** (The Transfiguration of Chirst) from the 8th century which celebrates its name day on August 6th.

Gennadi - Lachania - Plimmyri

The village of Gennadi (64 km. from Rhodes) lies south of the center of the Bay of **Gennadi** and comes after Kiotari. In antiquity it was the deme of Pedieon, one of the 12 demes of the state of Lindos. This beautiful village containes the lavishly decorated church of Ayia Anastasis of Romaia from the 6th century. The natural beauty of Gennadi is centered mainly on its marvelous mountain and its clean sea. A road heading west from Gennadi passes through the mountainous Vati and arrives at **Apollakia** on the west side of Rhodes. A turn-off to the left south of Gennadi leads to the village of Lachania. Here are the ruins of the church of St. Avakoum. The village has superb beaches, the most important one being **Plymmyri** which has a refuge for fishing. There are also many old monasteries, the best known being **Zoodochos Pigi** (Life-Giving Source).

The fishing village of Kiotari to the north of Gennadi bay.

Katavia - Prasonisi

*Seven km. after the turn-off to Plimmyri, and after passing through the settlements of Chochlaka and Ayios Pavlos, you reach the southermost village on Rhodes, **Katavia**.*

Near here is Katavia, center of the ancient deme of Katavioi.

For those who like more adventure they can continue on to the southernmost part of Rhodes, the Cape of Prasonisi.

It is 12 km. from Katavia along a dirt road. Prasonisi ("Green Island") is connected to the rest of the island of Rhodes by a strip of sand about 1,000 meters long. Depending on the direction of the wind one side of this strip of sand will always have a wind-whipped sea while the other will be calm.

Above: Prasonisi, the southernmost point of the island.

Below: The enormous Gennadi Bay.

LINDOS

History - The Acropolis - The traditional settlement
The beach - The small harbours

Lindos lies on the east coast of the island at a distance of 56 km. from the capital of Rhodes.

Lindos, like the old Town of Rhodes, is one of the monuments that has been declared subject to preservation and thus has been able to retain its traditional color. Daily, foreigners and Greeks take ex-cursions to admire this village and its acropolis and swim at its marvellous beaches. According to Homer, Lindos was built by the Dorians at the same time as Kameiros and Ialyssos in the 12th century B.C. Rhodes sent nine ships to the Trojan War and most probably they all came from Lindos. This fact shows that during that period Lindos was the most powerful town in Rhodes. The development of the town was due to its naval power. Its two harbors as well as its impregnable acropolis were unique on Rhodes. There is information that Lindos already had colonies by the 7th century and that it monopolized a large part of trade and

The acropolis of Lindos dominates its leeward bay. Lindos is a cosmopolitan summer resort of international conseguence.

shipping in the Mediterranean. The Lindians were the first to draw up a naval code of justice, later know as the Rhodian Naval Code. This was to become the basis of Roman naval justice and is even to be found at the core of modern maritime law. The Lindians were also great sculptors. Their bronze statues are famed for their incomparable craft. The famous Colossus of Rhodes was a bronze statue by the Lindian artist Chares. The town reached the height of its power in the 6th century B.C. particularly during the reign of Cleobulos who ruled for more than 40 years. Cleobulos is regarded as one of the Seven Sages of antiquity, primarily because he was the first to support the funding of public works by fund-raising drives among the citizens. The money from these drives was used to build the Temple of Athena in 550 B.C. and for the aqueduct which still survives at Krana and whose water flows from the spigot in the village square.

1. *The settlement of Lindos with its acropolis. 2. Typical courtyard gates on Lindos.   3. The beautiful*

indos. 4. Panoramic view of Lindos with its waterfront which is visited by dozens of yachts each day.

The traditional architecture and decoration is unique in all of Greece.

When the town of Rhodes was built in 408 B.C. quite a few inhabitants of Lindos moved to the New Town along with sculpture center and the shipyards. But Lindos still remained the center of maritime trade. The coming of the steamship contributed to the complete decline of the harbor which had already begun in the 18th century with the founding of other commercial stations.

In 1522 the Knights of St. John who controlled shipping and trade, abandoned the island and the Turks, who came immediately afterward, not having any knowledge of or interest in trade permitted the Lindians to organize commerce and shipping as they so desired. The village today has many houses from the 16th, 17th and 18th century known as "Captains' houses". Their architecture and decoration is unique in Greece. Until recently these houses were deserted but with the upsurge of capital from tourism the locals have been able to restore them under the supervision of the Archaeological Service thus preserving the traditional style of the town.

Between 1902 and 1912 the Archaeological School of Denmark carried out excavations on the acropolis and the surrounding area. The oldest finds that came to light were stone tools from the Neolithic period (3rd millennium B.C.) which proves how far back the history of Lindos stretches.

Among the most important finds in the area are two marble plaques which were inscribed by Timochidas, a priest of Athena, in 99 B.C. The one contains a list of the priests serving the goddess and the other is an account of her miracles accompanied by a list of the visitors to the temple and the gifts each one left.

The find, known as "The Chronicle of the Temple of Lindian Athena" confirms that several of the best known names in Greek history visited the temple. Among them are included Herakles, Helen of Troy and Menelaos, Artaphernes, King of Persia and Alexander the Great.

The **Acropolis** is a nearly triangular rock, 166 meters high, wider and shorter in the north section and four levels higher to the south. The walls that were built by the Knights dominate the top of the acropolis. The ancient walls were much lower and did not hide the buildings that were inside them.

Going through the entrance you climb up the stairway that leads to the first level. There are three underground reservoirs of water here and graneries from the Byzantine period. There is a magnificent view of the bay to your left. There are many pediments for statues and even more inscriptions. This is because during the Hellenistic period, rich visitors had the custom of making dedications to the goddess Athena. Despite the fact that there were so many statues here very few were found during the archaeological excavations. On this first level there are two very important monuments carved into the rock, an exedra and a trireme done in relief.

In 170 B.C., the Lindians, in order to pay their respects to Agesandros, carved the prow of his triereme into the rock, using its bronze statue as its base. At the bottom of the relief is an inscription, in poor condition, that states the town of Lindos awarded Agesandros a gold wreath. The exedra (platform), that has also been dug out of the rock, most probably belongs to the same period as the boat and was used by the nobles of Lindos as their headquarters.

An inscription from the 3rd or 4th century B.C. tells us that Aglochartos, was the one who handled the renovations on the temple. The temple stayed in operation until 396 A.D. when Theodosious II ordered the destruction of all the remnants of idololatry. The Olympic Games were also forbidden at that time. The priests of Lindian Athena were opposed to these directives and were subsequently sentenced to death.

The exedra with a ship in relief (trireme).

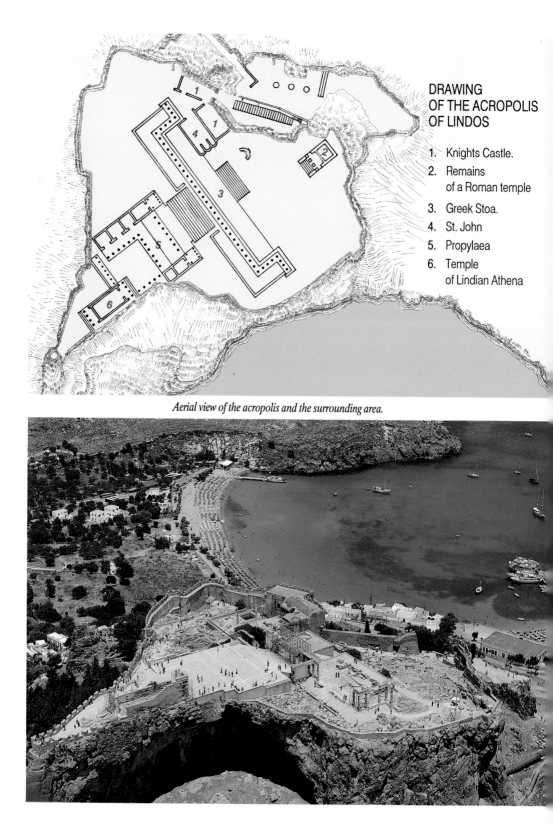

DRAWING OF THE ACROPOLIS OF LINDOS

1. Knights Castle.
2. Remains of a Roman temple
3. Greek Stoa.
4. St. John
5. Propylaea
6. Temple of Lindian Athena

Aerial view of the acropolis and the surrounding area.

The stairs leading up to the castle.

The Temple of Lindian Athena.

After the exedra and the relief trireme you go on to the steepest part of the acropolis. You will use the stairs that were built by the Knights which leads to the castle above the gate of which is the coat-of arms of the Grand Master d'Aubusson. The existence of this coat-of-arms shows that the castle was renovated at the end of the 15th century. A few stairs from the old staircase can still be see on your left as you ascend.

After the first room in the castle your turn left and pass through the second room and exit before a row of open-air storerooms. To the left there is another exedra which was used as a base for a statue and which, according to one theory, was the where novices were initiated into the mysteries of the worship of Athena. There are other bases for statues in the area while further left are the ruins of a Roman temple. The stairway, which is to the right, leads to the third level. Here there is a large **Hellenistic Stoa** in a U shape. It is is said this design was chosen because it resembled open hands welcoming pilgrims.

The stoa is dated to the 3rd century B.C., is 87 m. long and has 42 Doric columns along its facade. The reconstruction of the Stoa and the other ruins on the acropolis were carried out during the Italian occupation. In the northwest corner of the Stoa you will come upon the ruins of the Byzantine church of St. John.

The wide staircase leads from here to the **Propylaea**. It is sometimes called the "stairs to heaven" because it does give you the impression that you are mounting into the clouds.

At the top, on the forth level, is the reconstructed **Temple of Lindian Athena**. The temple is small, 22 meters long and only 8 wide but it merges so well into the natural environment and the arrangement of the buildings on the acropolis that if it were larger it would jar. The nature of the site forced the builders to use an unusual north-south axis.

According to an ancient myth, the first temple to be built on this site was the work of Danaos who fleeing from Egypt with his fifty daughters reached Lindos and was given hospitality by the Lindians. Contemporary scholars believe that the worship of the goddess Athena began during the 8th century. **The temple whose ruins you see today** was built during the middle of the 4th century on the ruins of the old one. In the center you can make out the base of the statue of Athena. That statue was made of marble, wood, gold and ivory and was listed among the masterpieces of Greek art. Emperor Theodosios II transferred the statue to Constantinople along with other temple treasures and there it was later destroyed. According to tradition the **harbor took its name from the Apostle Paul** who disembarked there during his visit to Lindos to preach the message of Christianity.

Below: the small harbor of Ayios Pavlos can be seen from the south side of this same cliff.

The **ancient theater** of Lindos lies to the right of the harbor. Several parts of its wedge-shaped seats and the orchestra have survived, as they were carved into the rock. West of the acropolis, on Krana hill, is the ancient cemetery. Most of the tombs have fallen into ruin with the passage of time with the exception of the family tomb of Archocrates from the 2nd century B.C. only the middle section of which has collapsed; it is a superb example of funerary architecture in Lindos.

The visit to the acropolis of Lindos is an unforgettable experience with a view toward the village, the sea, the two harbors and the island.

View of the acropolis and the settlement of Lindos; the theater can be seen beneath the acropolis.

Views of Lindos from the acropolis.

Descending from the acropolis and strolling through the lanes of the town with its many tourist shops *(foto 1)* the visitor should not leave out a visit to the **Church of Our Lady (Theotokou)** which is located near the village square. It was most probably built in the 14th century on the site of an older church. The Grand Master d'Aubusson renovated it in 1489 and built the **bell-tower on which his coat-of-arms can be seen** *(foto 2)*. The interior walls are decorated with well maintained wall paintings from 1799 while the carved wooden iconostasis and the bishop's throne are marvellous examples of wood-carving from the 17th century. The floor of the **church is decorated with black and white pebbles in a zigzag pattern** *(foto 3)*. This technique, known as "chochlaki" has its roots in the Hellenistic period and reached its zenith during the Byzantine period. Many examples, in a variety of designs, can be found throughout Rhodes.

View of Lindos.

1

10
THE WEST COAST

Ixia - Ialyssos - Filerimos
The Valley of the Butterflies - Tholos
Kameiros - Kritinia - Monolithos - Apolakia

The excursion along the western side of the island, which starts in the town of Rhodes and ends at the southernmost village on the island, Katavia, covers 110 km. and offers a wide range of things to enjoy. The cosmopolitan and well-regulated beaches of Ixia and Ialyssos, in combination with the important archaeological sites at Ialyssos and Kameiros, the medieval castles of Filerimos, Castello and Monolithos as well as the one and only Valley of the Butterflies make for an incomparable mixture of history, natural beauty and modern tourist development. If you want to complete this excursion in one day you should head along the west coast where you will only have time to cast a fleeting glance at all these sights and perhaps spend a bit longer at the archaeological sites of Ialyssos and Kameiros or wherever you find something of particular interest. You will also, of course, have the opportunity to visit the eastern part of the island. But you will need at least one or two days to do this properly because this kind of beauty takes a while to appreciate. During this excursion you will pass through the coastal areas of Ixia and Ialyssos with their luxurious hotel complexes. You will also visit Filerimos hill with the archaeological site of Ialyssos (the most ancient well-defined settlement on the island dating to 1500 B.C.) and you will be astonished of the spectacle of millions of butterflies swarming in their lovely valley. Then you will pass through the picturesque village of Tholos and head south toward ancient Kameiros. Continuing along this excursion you will move away from the shore and discover the other side of Rhodes, the central and south sections of the island with their well-tended produce, the green-capped mountains and the medieval castles of Castello and Monolithos with their unique views.

Kritika - Ixia

Using the town of Rhodes as your starting point you head west and on your left you will find a small settlement of incredibly beautiful houses. It is called **Kritika** ("Cretan neighborhood") and it took its name from its original settlers, who came from Crete in 1898. On the right is the bay of Trianda. Because of the strong north winds that blow here at the end of summer it is a cool and pleasant place during the hot days of July and August.

The large beach there is nearly 8 km. long and combines sand with large, white pebbles. This beach is called **Ixia** and has a large assortment of restaurants, commerical shops, night clubs and hotel complexes, most of which are luxury class and it is a place where socialites tend to gather.

Above: the settlement of Kritika.
Below and on opposite page: The cosmopolitan beach at Ixia on the enormous gulf of Ialyssos (Trianda).

Ixia.

Trianda

At the end of this bay is the village of Trianda which is on the exact same site as the Doric town of Ialyssos. Despite the fact that Trianda is in the middle of a cosmopolitan area that attracts a lot of tourists, it still retains the feel of Rhodian agricultural center. Its square is highlighted by the church of the Dormition of the Virgin built in the 17th century with a superb carved wooden iconostsasis made in 1810 and an extremely impressive belfrey. Nearby is the small church of Ayios Nikolaos with lovely wall paintings from the 15th century. Scattered throughout the area of Ialyssos are towers from the time of the Knights as well as neoclcassical mansions. During the first fortnight in August the Municipality holds the "Ialyssia" Festival where you can enjoy dancing and music performed by local groups, theatrical performances and a revival of local customs.

The peak of Filerimos hill above Trianda.

Ialyssos and Filerimos

In 1876 archaeologists found the necropolis of Ialyssos lyng between the village of Trianda and Filerimos hill. This is the most ancient well-defined settlement on the island (1550-1400 B.C.). Most of the finds are in the British Museum and the Louvre and only a few in the Rhodes Museum. Most of the priceless items, jewellery by and large, are from the 5th century B.C. which shows that the town reached its zenith then. In the ancient Greek world Ialyssos was famed for the athletic feats of the Eratides family, the leading figure being Diagoras who won the Olympic boxing competition three times. When he won for the third time in 464 B.C. Pindar wrote his 7th Olympic Ode in honor of him. After the town of Rhodes was built in 408 B.C. many of the inhabitants of Ialyssos moved there so that their own town began to slowly delcine. Turning left at Trianda and going 5 km. along a road through a dense pine forest you arrive at the top of Filerimos hill (267 m.). There is an amazing view from here. To the north is the bay of Ialyssos with its large hotels and to the west the villages of Kremasti and Paradeisi. To the south you can see the villages of Pastida and Maritsa, next to the old airport, and even further away, the thickly wooded Mt. Profitis Ilias along with the bare summit of Mt. Attavyros. This was the acropolis of Ialyssos which was used during the Byantine period and under the Knights for military purposes. In 1248 when the Genoese took Rhodes, the Byzantines withstood a siege there. It was also the first site to be fortified by the Knights when they settled on Rhodes in 1306. This is where Suleiman the Magnificent set up his headquarters during the great siege of 1522. During the Second World War the Italians installed their artillery batteries here.

The large harbor of Ialyssos in tbe bay of the same name.

The hill took its name from a monk who came from Jerusalem in the 13th century bringing with him an icon of the Blessed Virgin painted by the Apostle Luke. Today that icon is in St. Petersburg and a copy has been put in its place. The small church he built later became a baslica and then in the 14th century the Knights built in St. John, a large monastery dedicated to the Virgin Mary with its exquisite bell-tower that one still sees today. There is where the miracle-working icon is so reverently kept. The monastery was destroyed during the Turkish occupation. The Italians rebuilt the monastery during their occupation and kept it open with monks from the Capuchin Order. Behind the church are the monks' cells, the walls of which are decorated with mosaic depictions of saints. During the war the monks returned to Italy and since then the monastery has been closed. The main church of the monastery was more like a small chapel to the Virgin Mary and young couples had romantic weddings there.

Going up the ancient road to the acropolis, on your left below the church is the amphiprostyle temple of the Ialyssian Polias Athena from the 3rd century B.C. The temple was destroyed in the 6th century A.D. when its building material was used for the triple-aisled basilica of Filerimos. What is mainly left of this church is the Bapistry and the cruciform-shaped font with its two steps so that those about to be baptized may enter it. On your left as you face the anient monument is the church of Ayios Georgios (St. George) Chostos whose interior is completely covered wth superb wall paintings from the 14th-15th century using the technique developed by the Knights but with Byzantine influences while to your right is the monastery of the Blessed Virgin (Panayia).

Left of the square with the large oak trees are the ruins of a triple-aisled, cruciform church with a dome covered with wall paintings, a small main church (katoliko) of a Byzantine monastic complex from the 10th century. There is another road that sets off from the square that leads to the westernmost point of the hill. The **Road to Golgotha** used by the Catholics was dotted with holy icon-stands and bronze reliefs with representations of the Passion of Christ. There is a very impressive view from there.

Holy Shrine on the road to Golgotha.

Exiting through the iron gate of the archaeological site, a short distance away on your left a road leads to a well-preserved Doric fountain made of porous stone, from the 4th century B.C. Two conduits brought water from the mountain and deposited it in a small reservoir cut into the rock. The main building of the fountain was enclosed in front with a Doric colonnade. The water flowed out through marble spouts in the shape of a lion's head.

Above, left: the main church of the Monastery of the Blessed Virgin (Panayia) where romantic weddings are performed.

Below: the courtyard of the Filerimos Monastery.

Kremasti - Paradeisi

Heading southwest on the road from Trianda, 4 km. along you will reach **Kremasti** one of the largest and most vigorous villages on Rhodes. It is 12 km. from the town. It is a communications hub which connects the entire northern side of the island with the town and the airport with the eastern section by means of a new provincial road. It also combines greenery with a beautiful beach that is 700 meters from the community and occupies the site on which ancient Ialyssos stood. Its castle was built during the time of the Knights and was the residence of the Grand Masters; it is on a small hill in the middle of the settlement. The church of the Dormition of the Virgin Mary commands the area; it celebrates on the 15th of August and the nine holy days of the Blessed Virgin. This is a shrine shared by all the Dodecanese and the feast lasts from the 10 to the 23 of August.

During the same period the Panhellenia exhibition of handicrafts is held at Kremasti. Cultural events are also held on New Year's Day, the Epiphany and during Easter.
The village of **Paradeisi**, which comes after Kremasti, is 15 km. from the town. There is a theory that its name truly means a place of fruitfulness and fertility. The ruins of the fortress at the entrance to the village resting on top of a small plateau reveal that during the time of the Knights it was flourishing. In the village you can admire the impressive wooden iconostasis in the church of Ayios Nikolaos and the icons in all the many monasteries that abound, dating from the 14th century to the present day.
The Dormition of the Virgin Mary is celebrated in August with a large festival. View from Kremasti, one of the largest villages on Rhodes.

View from Kremasti, one of the largest villages on Rhodes.

Tholos (Theologos)

Continuing along the coast road to the southwest you will come to the picturesque village of **Tholos** (Theologos) three km. along the way, to your left, built on the slopes of a small hill. At its foot is a fertile band of land of over 2,000 meters, thickly planted with olive and fig trees and vineyards. The history of the area is lost in the depths of time. The "Deme of Istanion" was its ancient Greek name and its god was Helios, the "Erethimios Apollo" (The "Red Apollo"), whose temple was a major pole of attraction during the Hellenistic period; this was succeeded during Christian times by St. John the Divine. So the area was given a new name. Excavations have uncovered remanants of a Mycenean civilization beneath the Byzantine ruins.

Today Tholos is a small village which has its own unsullied beauty and has resisted the passage of time. It has hospitable inhabitants, narrow lanes, cozy houses, many of which are renovated but its main point of attraction is the church of Ayios Spyridonas (St. Spyridonas) which has a dazzling white bell-tower and an ancient tree in its courtyard. The ultramodern hotels there are perfect for an ideal, and hospitable, holiday while the sandy shores and the cool breezes of summer attract friends of marine sports. The area is also suitable for hiking in the hills. Each year on the 14th and 15th of August the community, along with its visitors, participates in the great festival at the **Kalopetra Monastery** in the verdant Valley of the Butterflies.

The church of Ayios Spyridonas.   *Colorful cafe.   Below: view of Tholos.*

The Valley of the Butterflies

Three km. from Paradeisi you turn to left and 6 km. later you reach the renowned **Valley of the Butterflies**, one of the most unusual biotopes in Europe. It is a luxuriant ravine with abundant running water that attracts thousands of tourists each summer.

A German entomologist, Rheinhard Eiger, visited the island a number of years ago and made a study of the butterflies that appear there from July to September. These butterflies belong to the species Callimorpha Qudripunctaria Himalaiensis because they were discovered for the first time in the Himalayas. It has been since learned that they also are found in Brazil, Peru, Australia, California and wherever else the Liquidabar Ortintalis trees are native, which have a resin with a distinctive, strong aroma.

The butterflies live in the valley during the summer, mate and fly away in September leaving their eggs at various points around the island. In April these eggs produce the small larva which are transformed into chrysales in May and achieve their final form at the beginning of June. When it turns hot they leave the locale where they were born and, travelling by night, reach the valley where they will stay until September. They are attracted by the smell of the resin as well as the coolness of the surroundings which does not change even during the hottest days of summer. Down deep at the bottom of the valley is a quaint restaurant built in an Alpine style.

A dirt road shrouded in greenery climbs up from the Valley of the Butterflies and two km. later reaches the **Kalopetra Monastery**. It was built in 1784 by the abbot of Wallachia, Alexandros Ypsilantis, who had then been sent into exile on Rhodes by the Turks.

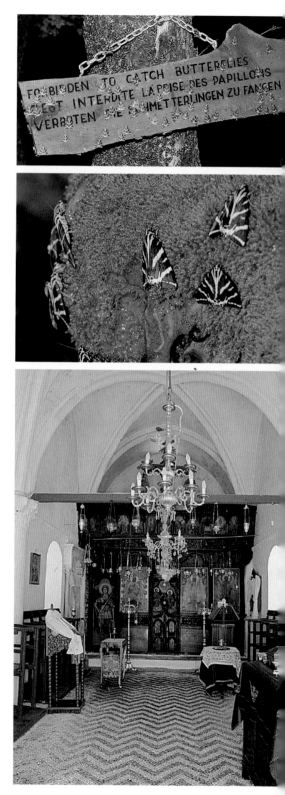

Above and right page:
From the Valley of the Butterflies.
Below: The Kalopetra Monastery nestled
in the verdant Valley of the Butterflies.

Soroni - Fanes - Kalavarda

Soroni lies three km. from the village of Tholos going left. The Monastery of Ayios Soulas is there. One of the most frequented festivals on the island is held there each year on July 30. In the afternoon there are athletic competitions, horse and donkey races conducted on the simplest of playing fields and in the evening dances. From Soroni an inland road goes through Dimylia and Archipoli (see Inland Excursions). **Fanes** with a small marina comes after Saroni.

At the village of **Kalavarda** (seven km. from Saroni and 30 km. from the town) the road divides. Left it goes into the interior of the island and right it is a continuation of the coast road which reaches ancient Kameiros after 4 km.

Traditional events in the village of Soroni.

Ancient Kameiros

Ancient Kameiros has been called the Pompey of Greece but it is a rather far-fetched parallel because Pompey, as is well-known, was buried in a dramatic fashion under the lava of Mt. Vesuvius while Kameiros was gradually abandoned by its inhabitants and was buried by the earth itself with the passage of time.

The town was founded by the Dorians, just like Ialyssos and Lindos. But the discovery of a Mycenean necopolis near the village of Kalavarda makes it clear that during the prehistoric period, before the descent of the Dorians, the area must have been inhabited by the Achaeans. Contrary to Lindos, which had a great naval tradition, Kameiros was by and large a rural society whose main products were olive oil, figs and wine. The need to export these products was the stimulus for the creation of a major cermaics industry. The town reached its greatest height in the 6th century B.C. which has been determined by the pottery that was found, in addition to the fact that during that same century Kameiros was the first Rhodian town to mint its own coins.

But when the town of Rhodes was founded in 408 B.C. the inhabitants of Kameiros began to leave their town. Archaelogical discoveries show that during the 4th century B.C. there was only a small town left on the site and this was later completely abandoned. A few centuries after that the area was reforested and was still known to the inhabitants of the neighboring villages as "Kameiros". This name and the chance discovery of a number of tombs by the villagers, led the archaeologists Biliotti and Salzmann to do excavations in the area. Their first discvery was the necropolis on the surrounding hills. There was a wealth of finds, pottery in the main with which the inhabitants of the ancient town even decroated their tombs. Most of these objects have been transferred to the British Museum and to the Louvre.

View of ancient Kameiros.

As you enter the archaeological site you will see the **Agora** (Market) in front of you and a sanctuary to a still unidentified god. Northwest of the sanctuary are the ruins of a **Doric temple** from the 3rd century B.C. two columns of which have been rebuilt; right next to this temple is a practically **square** that is practically square with three stiarways: on the east, northeast and southeast sides. Perhaps this is the place where the faithful sat and listened to the priests perform their liturgy in front of the temple. In the southern part of the temple there are the ruins of a **reservoir** which handled the needs of the market. In front of this there are a row of restored columns.

Moving toward the stairway that leads to the town's main street, on your right you will see a semicircular **exedra** perhaps used for speeches or announcements. Throughout antiquity the agora was the commerical, social and political center of the island.

Behind this platform is a walled-in rectangular space which is where the altars to the gods were and where sacrifices took place.

Near the northern section of the main street, which divides the area into two parts, you will see the **public baths** which were built in imitation of Roman baths. Next to the baths is a cistern. As you go up you will see private dwellings both left and right. The land becomes steeper as you near the acropolis.

The **acropolis** occupies a triangular and flat piece of ground (120 meters in area) at the top of the hill. Practically its entire north side is covered by the **Large Stoa**, resting on two rows of Doric columns. Behind them is a series of rooms. The Large Stoa was erected in the 3rd century B.C. on top of an enormous reservoir, built in the 6th century by cutting into the soft stone of the acropolis. This reservoir held 600 cubic meters of rain water which ran off the roofs of the buildings on the acropolis. The water reached the down by a sophisticated system of pipes which were originally made of stone and later of clay. Behind the Stoa there was a temple to Athena built at the end of the 3rd century B.C.,

on the site of an older temple which was destroyed by an earthquake in 226 B.C. The acropolis has a captivating view of the town, the sea, the samller islands and the coast of Asia Minor. You can also swim on the beach at ancient Kameiros.

Detail from the archaeological site of Kameiros.

Skala Kameiros

Skala Kameiros is 16 km. to the southwest and was most probably the harbor of Kameiros. Today it is a picturesque little fishing harbor. Every morning caiques leave there and in one and half hours reach the neighboring **island of Chalki.**

The beach at Skala Kameiros.

The archaeological site of Kameiros with a good beach for swimming to the rear.

Castello - Kritinia - Attavyros

Continuing south the road goes uphill to a verdant mountain. A road to the right leads to the Castle of Castello which was built by the Knights of Rhodes at the beginning of the 16th century to protect the west coast of the island. The castle is of a Byzantine and medieval design and inside are the ruins of the Catholic church of St. Paul. Going on up the main road you pass through a gorgeous landscape with a panoramic view of the islands of **Chalki, Alymia, Makri, Strongyuli** and **Tragousa**. Five km. past Skala Kameiros you come to the village of Kritinia, clinging to the side of a mountain. It took its name from its earliest inhabitants, who were Cretans. As soon as you reach the village you will see Mt. **Attavyros** the highest mountain on Rhodes (1,215 m.). According to mythology, Althaimenis, the grandson of Minos, the King of Crete, came to Rhodes and set up a colony at Kritinia. Since he was homesick for his native land he built a glorious temple on the summit of the mountain in honor of Attavyrios Zeus so that he could gaze at Crete from there. All the slopes and ridges of the mountain are green with pine forests and vineyards while the summit is completely barren. Originally the settlement was at the seaside at the site of Skala Kameiros but during the post-Byzantine period it was moved to the mountains to make it more secure from pirates. The settlement is also protected by the Castle of Castello. There is a Folklore Museum in the Village. The road divides five km. after Kritinia. The left branch goes to Ebonas (see p. 144,) six km. away, while if you go straight ahead you will reach south Rhodes.

Akramitis - Sianna

You follow the main road and continue south for 9 km. through pine forests with a panoramic view of the west coast of the island and the neighboring islets; you then arrive at the small village of Sianna at the foot of Mt. Akramitis, the second highest on Rhodes (825 m.).

The Byzantine medeval castle of Castello.

Sianna, nestled in a dense green forest, produces high quality honey as well as "souma", a kind of ouzo made of distilled grapes. This is the spot for those who want a quiet holiday and a place from which to take walks and explore a natural environment practically untouched by any kind of development.

Monolithos - Apolakia - Skiadi Monastery

Five km. from Sianna is the village of **Monolithos** which is also on the slopes of Mt. Akramitis and which faces Karpathos while on the other side Mt. Attavyros and the interior of the island can be seen. The village is a combination of the dark green mountain and the clean sea, archaeological sites and Byzantine monasteries with wall paintings. The hospitable inhabitants serve you only the finest local produce. Following a road that goes down to the sea you will reach, after one km. the medieval **Castle of Monolithos** built on the top of a rock. It is one of the most noteworthy sites on Rhodes not so much because of the buildings in the castle as for its imposing position. Here you can savor unique sunsets and a superb view of the sea and the interior of the island. Inside the castle there is a small church dedcated to Ayios Panteleimonas, probably built in the 15th century.

The road that goes to the sea divides after one km.: to the right it goes to Monastery of **Ayios Georgios** (St. George) and left to the beach of **Fournoi** where there is a tranquil combination of pine forests and sandy beaches with sparkling blue water.

The road goes from the village of Monolithos to the more southern villages. 10 km. along you reach the village of **Apolakia**. **Katavia** is 17 km. from there. The road, which is right next to the sea, wanders through fields of wheat, and various kinds of melons between low sand dunes. Five km . after Apolakia you can turn and go up the road through a wonderful pine forest which after 4 km. leads you to the **Skiadi Monasterty**. The monastery is from the 18th century and has a view of the coatline.

The medieval castle of Monolithos located on an imposing site.

11

INLAND EXCURSIONS

Kalavarda - Salakos - Apollonas - Dimylia
Maritsa - Ebonas - Ayios Isidoros - Istrios

Rhodes is not only its old town, its beautiful, cosmopolitan beaches, its seaside villages and its historical monuments; there is also the island's interior with its lush natural environment, the verdant mountains and the picturesque little villages still untouched by thr waves of tourists who have flooded the island. On this excurison you will get to know a considerable number of the 44 villages that make up Rhodes and that are scattered over the whole the island; once more you will experience the genuine hospitality of the inhabitants. You will sample their traditional produce and enjoy the healthy climate in combination with the unique physical landscape. One of the interesting excurisons you can take sets off from the village of Kalavarda on the west coast and ends at the settlement of Kolybia on the east coast, passing through enchanting landscapes and picturesque villages. Outside the main part of this excursion there are also a number of shorter trips to make. One turn-off sets off from the village of Archopoli and cuts across the north part of the island ending at Ialyssos and the town of Rhodes and another excursion follows the road which sets off from the village of Salakos and heads south to take in Mt. Attavyros and then crosses the south central section of the island. Here you will have the chance to meet the real Rhodians with their traditional costumes and their spontaneous ways. In the traditional village of Ebonas, famed for its intense folk character and its good wine, festivals are organized during the summer in which local costumes are worn and visitors are invited to take part. The excursion that will cover all these inland villages on Rhodes cannnot be reduced to terms of kilometers because the roads in the interior of the island are continually branching this way and that and it all depends exclusively on the mood and the adventuresome spirit of the visitor just how far he will push into the interior of the island in order to enjoy the beauty of the natural landscape and the peace and quiet so generously afforded by these areas.

Salakos - Profitis Ilias

You follow the road along the west coast up to the village of Kalavarda (30 km.). Eight km. further south, at the foot of Mt. Profitis Ilias you will reach the village of **Salakos**, which has an abundance of water and lush vegetation. The water from the Nymphi spring supplies water to the town of Rhodes. Just before the spring a path leads to the summit of **Profitis Ilias** which is a twenty minute walk. The mountain is verdant with thick stands of cypress and pine. On the first plateau on this excursion you will see the church of the Archangel Michael and on the second the church of the Prophet Elijah (Profitis Ilias) at the very top of the mountain (798 m.). There are two traditional hotels here built by the Italians, "Elafos" and "Elafina" ("Stag" and Doe) but they have been closed for the past few years. You can still stop and enjoy the view.

Right: the traditional Elafos hotel.
Below: view of Salakos with its abundant water.
Right page, above: the church of Profitis Ilias and below: a
traditional hotel on top of a mountain with a splendid view.

Apollonas - Eleousa - Dimylia

The road from Salakos continues south and after 6 km. a turn-off to the left (if you are driving) leads to the peak of Profitis Ilias that we have already described. Another turn-off a bit further along the main road leads to Ebonas (see p. 144).

On the road leading inland you will often encounter scenes that remind you of the traditional everyday way of life.

Coming back down the road and heading east you enter a dense stand of pine, and ideal place for the Rhodian deer.

You the arrive at the village of **Apollonas** where the ruins of a temple to Apollo, who was worshipped here, have been found. The large number of plane trees in the area lent their name to the small village of **Platania** (Platanos = plane tree). The road heading north reaches the settlement of **Eleousa** which belongs to the community of **Dimylia** a small village nestled in dense shrubbery, 2 km. further north. Eleousa has the church of Ayios Charalambos (formerly Catholic) and the **Monastery of Ayia Eleousa**.

Fountoukli - Archipoli

*There is the Byzantine church of Ayios Nikolaos(St. Nikolas) on the site of **Fountoukli**, two kilometers from Eleousa. This is a stone church from the 13th century with four apses and unique Byzantine paintings from the 14th century. You can enjoy the view from here and quench your thirst with the cool water from the spring outside the church.*

*After the quaint village of Eleousa the road heads east to **Archipoli**. This is a mountain village with abundant water and fertile soil where the inhabitants are primarily concerned with farming and animal husbandry and less with tourism. The road heading east reaches the **Ayios Nektarios Monastery** which lies in a beautiful setting of trees and shrubs and running water. Epta Piges and Kolybia, which are on the east coast, are not far from here.*

Psinthos - Maritsa

*Going north on the road from Archipoli you reach the village of **Psinthos**. The road branches at this point; if you turn to the left you will go to the Valley of the Butterflies while if you turn right you will reach the areas of Afantou and the village of Kalythies on the leeward side. If you take third road to the north you will reach the village of **Maritsa** after about 8 km. There are many country chapels in the area with wall paintings in a variety of styles and there are also two windmills which have been declared subject to preservation. The dominant feature in this village with its old houses is the bell-tower of the Church of Taxiarchs. The town of Rhodes is 17 km. from Maritsa.*

To get to know south-central Rhodes you start from the traditional village of Ebonas and take the road south from Salakos or go east after Kritinia along the east coast.

Above: The Byzantine church of St. Nikolas) at Fountoukli.

Below: Events around Maritsa.

Ebonas - Ayios Isidoros

Ebonas lies at the foot of Mt. Attavyros. It is the main village in the area with many vineyards and is famed for its high quality wine. There are wine cellars here as well as a number of tavernas and tourist shops. The village has many folkloric features and the locals still wear their traditional dress. During the summer events are staged which include dances where tourists are invited to join in. South of Ebonas the road winding through the lush green shade and clinging to Mt. Attavyros arrives 12 km. later at **Ayios Isidoros**, a mountainous village 65 km. from the town. Ayios Isidoros, at a height of 532 m. and built on the eastern slopes of Mt. Attavyros has not been influenced by tourism and has preserved all its traditions, especially those connected with Easter. Visitors will enjoy the healthy climate, the hospitality of the inhabitants and the village's own produce such as the wine, honey, the ouzo-like "souma" and the olive oil.
There is a path from the village which after a two hour hike leads to the top of Mt. Attavyros (1,215 m.). There is a small church to St. John there, which has fallen into ruin.

Laerma - Istrios

After Ayios Isisdoros you reach the village of **Laerma** whch takes it name from the "people of Hermes" ("laos of Hermes") the god that was worshipped there during antiquity.
Further south on a plateau (280 m. high) and 85 km. from the townof Rhodes is the village of **Istrios**. This is a cool, refreshing area and is also a biotope -- a refuge for partridge, hare and deer. In the center of the village is a large church dedicated to Ayios Nektarios with a carved wooden iconostasis, a pebbled floor and the icon of the saint illustrated by a Cretan painter. This is a place to enjoy the green countryside, the peace and quiet, the running water and the sunset over the mountains of Karpathos. You can return to the town from Istrios along the east coast by way of Gennadi or along the west coast by way of Apolakia.

LET THE FUN BEGIN

Sports - Markets and Dining - Night Life
Excursions to Neighboring Islets

The cosmopolitan and at the same time so attractive island of Rhodes offers its visitors a practically countless number of choice, whether they prefer a life close to nature mixed in with a variety of athletic activities or are more attracted by the night life and its entertainments. The island is always at your service and is equally prepared to reveal its natural charms to you as well as its ultramodern tourist facilities. This is why Rhodes is one of the leading tourist resorts in the world. People stream there from all parts of the world in order to glory in its golden sun, its deep blue sea, its

The island is always at your service and is equally prepared to reveal its natural charms to you as well as its ultramodern tourist facilities.

ancient and medieval monuments as well as the hospitality of its inhabitants. In the following pages you will find useful information on all the things that might be of interest to you in regard to the athletic activities on the island, its markets and its night life, its fine dining and the excursions you can enjoy to the islands that lie just off Rhodes, such as the beautiful Chalki which has become an international center for youth, the picturesque Symi, with its traditional architecture and tranquil Tilos with its amazingly pristine beaches and open-hearted and hospitable residents.

Sports

Swimming

This is the most popular sport on Rhodes. There is always a choice of either sandy or rocky baches, calm waters or rough waves, beaches that are crowded or deserted. You can also swim, of course, in the pools that all the large hotels have.

Water-skiing

All the well-known beaches on the island have the propr equipment for this sport.

Wind-surfing

Wind surfers can rent their equipment at all the large beaches, as well as in the town. The east coast is suitable for beginners while the waves on the west coast are a challenge for the more experienced.

Sailing

The good weather on Rhodes from April to October make this an ideal site for this sport. Sailboats and motor-boats of various sizes are for rent at Mandraki. Whoever wishes to rent a boat should apply at the Sailing Club of Mandraki.

Underwater Fishing

Spear-fishing is a popluar sport in Rhodes and anyone over 18 can enjoy it.

Tennis

In the town, the Tennis Club o Rhodes is near the beach right outside the Naval Society. Moreover, many of the large hotels outside of town have their own tennis courts.

Golf

There is a large golf course in the village of Afantou, 19 kilometers from the town. It has dressing-rooms and a salon, a bar and a restarant as well as ashop with golf equipment.

Markets

There is perhaps no other town in the world the size of Rhodes that has so many shops.
The best one sell mainly leather goods, furs, ceramics, handifracafts and rugs.
The development of tourism on Rhodes attracted a large number of furriers to the town. They have their own worshop where you can order your own particular fur or leather jacket which you will receive in a few days time.
The town also has many boutiques and clothing shops which have the most fashionable goods at affordable prices. Customs rates on Rhodes date to 1948.
The inhabitants of Rhodes are well-known for their skill at silverwork, pottery-making, rug-weaving and other handicrafts.

Those who are interested can visit pottery worskshops which line the roads to Lindos and Kameiros. The villages of Afantou and Archangelos produce carpets of the highest quality whch can be ordered from the workshops in the village. The shops on Rhodes also have a large variety of purses, bags, blouses and other items with depictions of the island useful as a souvenir of your visit to the island.

Shopping in the numerous stores of Rhode is a pleasant way of passing time.

Dining

Good food and good drink contribute to one's enjoyment of a vacation on Rhodes. Rhodian cuisine is a combination of Greek imagination and European and Middle Eastern taste. The old town of Rhodes is filled with tavernas that exclusively serve fish and seafood. Tavernas that serve meat are usually to be fobnd in the suburbs and the nearby villages. The restaurants serve international cuisine as well as Greek. The town of Rhodes has Chinese, Danish and Cypriotrestaurznts while for those who prefer more romantic surroundings there are the medieval buildings in the old town which have been transformed into luxury restaurants fo dining by candle-light. There is also a floating restaurant at Mandraki, with the Knights Castle in the background, illuminated in summer.

The warm and friendly atmosphere is often accompanied by singing and dancing. You can also enjoy one of the large variety of famous wines produced by the wineries on the island.

On Rhodes you will find many pastry shops that serve Greek and Europran pastries. You can also play backgammon and cards in the island's cafes. Ouzo, wine and hors d'oeuvres are served there as well as coffee.

The Old Town has some of the most beautiful of the traditional cafes.

Night-Life

Besides its historical monuments and superb beaches Rhodes also has a thrillling night life to offer each of its visitors. The cosmopolitan atmosphere of Rhodes peaks during the evening. From the moment when the sunset spreads its peaceful colors all around, Rhodes becomes a poem.

There are many night-clubs with Greek music. There are also many dancing spots in the town with both Greek and foreign music. The music is usually live and the program often includes traditional dances. For the younger visitors there are many discos, both inside and outside the town.

You can attend performances of traditional dances at the outdoor theater in the Old Town, ancient tragedy and comedy at the ancient Stadiumn, concerts of classical music put on by the National Theater as well as the works of modern Greek composers.

The Sound and Light shows held in the lavsh garden of the Knights Palace depict the fall 0f Rhodes to the Turks through a superb blending of word, sound and light. These performances are given every evening in Greek, English, German, Swedish and French. The town also has a number of movie houses.

You can also visit the casino at the Grand Hotel. There you will find roulette, blackjack and chemin de fer as well as various kinds ofslot machines. Anyone over 21 is alllowed in, after showing a valid identity card or passport.

Rhodes also has a thrillling night life to offer each of its visitors

Excursions to the nearby Islands

Chalki

The small islands around Rhodes make for a pleasant change from the intense and cosmopolitan life on the island. There where the main source of income is still from the sea, the simple and carefree way of life has changed little over the last few decades.

If you decide to explore them all you have to do is go to the harbor and take one of the caiques or other boats which depart from there regularly. The nearest island is **Alimia** which is opposite Skala Kameiros on the west coast. There are day trips from Skala Kameiros and the trip takes about 30 minutes. The small pebbled bay surrounded by pine trees also has the churches of Ayios Minas and Ayios Georgios. Moreover there is a medieval castle on the island from the time of the Knights of Rhodes. The island of **Chalki** is on the same side; it has been proclaimed an island of peace and friendship for the youth of all the world. A communal inn has been built for that purpose. The uninhabited islands that ar scattered around it give it a unique flavor all its own.

Symi lies to the northwest; its has many deep indentations, a rich tradition in mythology, houses in a grand architectural style, a castle, and small museums and monasteries that will leave you with indelible memories. Finally, further to the west is **Tilos**, between Symi and Chalki, which will sweep you away with its sparkling beaches and the warm hospitality of its inhabitants.

Chalki lies to the west of Rhodes, 35 nautical miles from the harbor but only 10 nautical miles from Skala Kameiros. It is one of the smallest islands in the Dodecanese: 28 sq. km with a coastline of 34 km. Chalki is beautiful and primitive with pristine sand beaches, crystal-clear water and few people, even though it is the the closest island to bustling Rhodes.

A mountainous and rocky island it has tourists in the summer who come from Rhodes.

The name Chalki comes from the Greek word for copper ("chalkos") which once existed on the island.

Nimborio. This is the capital of the island and lies on its east coast in a bay that is protected by an island at its entrance. Built on the slopes of the surrounding hills it gives the impression of a large, deserted town because most of its houses are abandoned. Down at the harbor is the noteworthy church of **Ayios Nikolaos** (St. Nikolas) with its magnifcent bell-tower.

Right nearby is the sand beach of **Pondamos**. The same is true of **Ftenagia** beach while a third beach is located on the islet of **Alimia**.

A cement road takes you to **Palio Chorio** after 2.5 km. This is the old capital of the island. now in ruins, lying at the foot of an imposing rocky hill. At the top of the hill can be seen the walls of a **Venetian castle**. There is a church dedicated to St. Nikolas inside the walls, with wall paintings.

The roads continues on to the west and after 3.5 km. arrives at the monastery of **Ayios Ioannis** (St. John).

Yialos with its harbor and Ano Syn

Symi

CHONDRO · NIMOS
PLATI
Emporio · Agia Marina
SYMI ⚓ Pedi
Roukounioti
Agios
DIAVATES Georgios
Marathounta
Panormitis
Faneromeni
SEKLI

Symi lies northwest of Rhodes, 21 nautical miles away. It covers an area of 58 sq. km. and its coastline is 85 km. long.

Mythology says that the god Glaucos abducted Symi, the daughter of the King of Ialyssos on Rhodes, and brought her to this island to which she was also to give her name.

Symi is one of the most picturesque islands in the Dodecanese with mountains that plunge straight down to the sea and fashion captivating bays. **Ano Symi** or **Chorio** as the local call it is located in one of these; it sweeps up the sides of two hills, to the right and left of the harbor, going all the way to the top of one and is a self-contained town on its own.

The quaintness, the tradtional architecture, the neoclassical houses with their pediments, the pebbled courtyards, all of which are creations of the 19th century, are quite impressive.

At the begining of the 20th century Symi has 30,000 inhabitants and was the capital of the Dodecanese and at the same time the largest sponge-fishing center in th world.

Ano Symi or **Chorio**. Ano Symi is the rather grand capital of the island which is how it appears when one comes in by boat.

The houses begin at **Kato Poli** (The "Lower Town" also called **Yialos** with its secure harbor)and go all the way up the hill to **Kastro** and the **Megali Panayia (The Blessed Virgin in her Magnificence)**.

You go up from the square at the landing stage climbing the 500 wide stairs of the **"Kali Strata"** (The "Good Street"). Right and left are the beautiful old houses with their neoclassical features.

A paved road sets off from Chorio and heads south, goes through a small forest of wild cypress trees and offers you an amazing view from its top. This road ends at the renowned **Panormitis Monastery** located at the southern tip of the island.

This is the most important monastery on the island and the second most important in the Dodecanese after the Monastery of St. John the Divine on Patmos. It is dedicated to the **Archangel Michael** and its main church has an icon of the saint done in gold.

Pedi. A seaside settlement, 2 km. east of Ano Symi to the rear of a neighboring sandy bay.

Emboreios. A small harbor, Symi's other one.

Excursions by Caique

During the summer caiques leave Yialos on day trips going to the island's marvelous beaches.

Ayios Aimilianos. A very picturesque beach. It is an islet with a church on it. A strip of rock connects the main island to the islet.

Ayios Vasileios. A gorgeous beach.

Ayia Marina. A rocky little island near Yialos.

Ayios Georgios Disalonas. This is probably the most spectacular beach on the island because behind there is an enormous rock 300 m. high.

Tilos

MEGALO CHORIO
Agios Panteleimonas
Livadia
Mikro Chorio

ANTITILOS

Tilos lies between Nisyros and Chalki; it has an area of 63 sq. km. and a coastline of 63 km. It has rocky soil with the exception of one small fertile valley in the approximate middle of the island, which ends at the beautiful sand beach of **Erystos**.

You can take a ferry-boat from Rhodes to Tilos.

Livadia. This is the port of Tilos set in a pebbled bay with sparkling clean water. This is a settlement with only a few inhabitants but it does have one large edifice built by the Italians which retains a few features of local architecture. To the northwest of Livadia is the deserted **Mikro Chorio** ("Little Village") with a number of interesting churches.

Megalo Chorio. This is the impressive capital of Tilos built at the base of a rocky hill with a castle perched at the top. Until the begining of the 18th century the village was inside the castle. There is where the old **Church of the Taxiarch** was built, on the foundations of an ancient temple. Among the things to be seen in the small village museum are the bones of a dwarf elephant from the **Charkadios Cave**. Two km. northwest of the renowned **Erystos** sand beach is the small harbor of Ayios Antonios. The road goes along the lovely Plaka sand beach and arrives at the **Ayios Panteleimonas** monastery. This monastery, dedicated to the patron saint of the island, is built in a small, verdant ravine with a spring and a panoramic view of the sea. It is 13 km. north of Livadia and was founded in the 15th century; it has wall paintings from 1776 and a beautiful courtyard laid with pebbles. It celebrates on July 27.

The renowned Panormitis Monastery

How to get to Rhodes
By plane
You can go to Rhodes by plane of Olympic Always departing from Athens ("El. Venizelos Airport) tel. (+30) 210 3530000. The trip takes about 50 minutes. You can also fly to Rhodes from the islands of Crete and Santorini: Olympic Airways Athens, tel. (+30) 210 9269111. The International Airport of Rhodes is one of the best in Greece. It lies in a distance 15 km. from the town, on the island's west coast, next to the village of Paradeisi. Contact Olympic Airways Rhodes, tel. (+30) 22410 83400. Rhodes Airport, tel. (+30) 22410 887000. Aegean Airlines: This line has flights year round from Athens' Airport (a flight of about one hour and 15'). Information, tel. (+30) 210 6261000. Charters: The airport at Rhodes has daily charter flights from many west European cities, as well as Cyprus, Tel Aviv and Cairo. In order to serve you better the airport has offices of the National Tourist Organization (EOT), a bank, automobile rental agencies, shops, a bar and for those going abroad, a duty-free shop. The airport is connected to the town by buses of Olympic Airways, which are synchronized with the flights. Those who are traveling in groups will be taken to Rhodes by the buses run by the tourist agencies.

By Sea
Large ferryboats go daily between Piraeus and Rhodes. Contact the Harbor Master's Office of Piraeus, tel. (+30) 210 4226001-3. Usually the ferryboats from Athens stop at the islands of Patmos, Leros, Kalymnos and Kos. Rhodes is also connected to the rest of the Dodecanese, as well as Crete, by smaller boats. Just recently direct boats from Piraeus to Rhodes have come into service, and since 1992 there have been connections with Thessalonica. At least once a week there is a large ferryboat that also goes to Limassol (Cyprus), Haifa (Israel), Alexandria (Egypt) and Ancona (Italy).

Transport
In order to get to know the countryside and the beaches of Rhodes, that are not part of the main excursions, you can make use of a good road network which connects the west and east coasts and goes through all the villages in the interior of the island. But the signs on the roads are not as good as they could be, particularly on the secondary roads and this requires caution; do not hesitate to ask for information from any villagers you meet. These people are always very willing to help you. You can make all these excursions by car, motorbike or even by bicycle if you have faith in your endurance. But using the buses of the tourist agencies or even by ordinary public bus can also do them. The most important beaches on the east coast, all the way to Lindos, can be reached by caique on day trips. There are also taxis, and a number of places to rent motorbikes and cars. There are also many petrol stations in the island's main town and in the larger villages.

Where to Stay
Depending on what you want and the means at your disposal, there are a wide variety of hotels of all categories to be found, with rooms or suites, pensions, and rooms to rent in private houses. There are no organized camping sites on Rhodes at the moment except for Faliraki camping. Camping on one's own is not allowed at anyplace on the island. July and August are the busiest months and it is not wise to come to Rhodes then without having booked a room in advance. But if for some reason you do come to Rhodes without having provided yourself with lodging you should go to the offices of the National Tourist Organization (EOT), tel. (+30) 22410 44330 or the Tourist Police, tel. (+30) 22410 27423. You can also get detailed hotel information from the Union of Hotel Owners of Rhodes, tel. (+30) 22410 74559.

Hotels of Rhodes

Rodos (22410)

Hotel	Class	Tel
ACANDIA	B	22251
ACHILLION	C	22391
ADONIS	C	27791
AEGAION	C	22491
AEGLI	C	22789
AGLA	B	22061
ALEXANDROS	B	34196
ALEXIA	B	24061
ALS	C	22481
AMARYLLIS	C	24522
AMBASSANDER	C	30431
AMPHITRYON	B	26880
ANASTASIA	D	21815
ANDREAS	B	28489
ANGELA	B	24614
AQUA MARIN	C	32669
AQUARIUS	B	27608
ARIS	E	23312
ASTRON	C	28996
ATHINA	B	22631
ATHINEON	A	26112
ATLANTIS	C	24821
ATTIKI	E	27767
AVRA BEACH	A	96284
BEACH HOTEL	B	23857
BELVEDERE	A	89000
BLUE SKY	A	24091
BUTTERFLY	C	75392
CACTUS	B	26100
CAMELOT	B	26549
CAPITOL	B	78821
CARINA	C	22381
CASA ANTICA	B	26206
BELLA VISTA	B	29900
CASTRO	E	20446
CAVO D' ORO	B	74154
CHEVALIERS PALACE	A	22781
CITY CENTER	B	36612
CONGO	C	28977
CONSTANTIN	B	22971
CONTINENTAL	A	30873
CORALLI	B	24912
DESPO	B	22571
DIANA	C	24667
DOMUS	E	25965
DORIAN	D	31796
KRITI	E	79131
KYPRIOTIS	C	35921
LA LUNA	E	25856
LEFKA	C	36792
LIA	E	26209
KAMIROS	A	22591
FLORA	C	77909
FLORIDA	C	22111
ERODIA	B	31361
ESAIAS APRTS	A	29408
ESPERIA	B	023941
EUROPA	B	24810
EL GRECO	C	24071
EMMANOUEL	B	22892
EMPONA	C	24139
EVA APRTS	A	29508
FEDRA	C	22791
FOUR SEASONS	C	31066
GALAXY	C	30007
GEORGE	B	21964
GOLDEN SUN APRTS	A	63983
GOLDEN SUN RISE	C	43003
GRAND HOTEL PALACE	A	54700
HELENA	C	24755
HELIOS APRTS	A	30033
HERMES	C	26022
IBISCUS	A	24421
ILIANA	E	30251
IMPALA	C	36856
INTERNATIONAL	C	24595
INTEUROPA	B	30642
KALHLUA	C	24488
LOMENIZ	B	35770
LOTUS	B	37221
LYDIA	C	22871
MAJESTIC	C	22031
MANISKAS	C	37412
MANOUSOS	B	22741
MARCO POLO	A	25562
MARIE	B	30595
MARIETTE	C	34593
MEDITERRANEAN	A	24661
MIMOZA	C	20432
MIRAGE	A	37417
MOSCHOS	C	24764
NAFSIKA	C	73040
NEW VILLAGE INN	E	34937
NEW YORK	C	22841
NIKOS - TINA	AA	34937
NISIA	D	20682
NOUFARA	C	24545
PANORAMA	B	37540
PARIS	D	26356
PARTHENON	C	22351
PAVLIDES	C	20281
PEARL	C	22420
PHAROS	E	28279
PHILOXENIA	C	37244
PLAZA	A	22501
PRINCESS FLORA	B	62010
RAINBOW	C	75506
REGINA	A	22171
RIVIER	A	22581
RODOS PARK	A	77140
ROYAL	C	31672
S. NIKOLIS	E	34561
SANDY COAST	C	73560
SARONIS	C	22811
SAVOY	C	20721
SEVA'S	D	26213
SEVEN PALMS	D	36830
SIRAVAST	A	23551
SEMIRAMIS	C	20741
SOLARIS	D	30611
SPARTALIS	C	24371
SPOT	E	34737
ST. ANTONIO	C	24971
STAR	D	30611
STATHIS	E	24357
STEVY	A	66031
STEVE	C	24498
SUNNY	C	33030
SUNRISE	B	30009
SYLVIA	C	22551
SYMI	E	23917
TILOS	C	24591
VASSILIA	C	35239
VENUS	C	29990
VIA - VIA	E	77027
VICTORIA	C	24626
VILLA RHODOS	C	20614
XANTHI	D	24996
ZEPHYROS	D	22826
ZEUS	E	23129
ELIT	C	22391
GONDOLA	C	86877
HERCULES	C	85002
IDEAL	C	85518
IKAROS	E	86287
IRINA	B	86070
K. SOTRILIS	D	86070
KOSTAS	C	85520
LIDO STAR	C	87754
LYMPERIA	C	85676
MARAN	C	86108
MARIANA	E	85238
MATINA	C	85813
MODUL	B	85548
MOUSSES	B	85303
NATASA	C	85507
NEFELI	E	85658
NEST	E	85390
ODYSSIA	E	85288
PLATANOS	E	85570
PLATON	D	85229
REA	E	85221
RENA	E	85120
RODANIA	C	85903
SEA VIEW	C	85903
SEMELI	C	85423
SOFIA	C	85003
ST. AMON	E	85430
STEVE	E	86448
SUN PALACE	A	85650
TELCHINES	C	85025
TIVOLI	C	47691
TSAMPIKA	C	85760
VENETIA	C	85612
VIOLETTA	B	85501

Faliraki (22410)

Hotel	Class	Tel
ACHOUSA	B	85970
ALOE	C	86146
ANASTA	C	85311
ANTONIOS	E	87100
APOLLO BEACH	A	85535
ARGO	C	85461
ATALANTI	B	85980
CAMPANA	E	85281
CATRHIN	A	85080
CHRISOULA	E	85660
DAFNI	E	85544
DANAE	B	85969
DIMITRA	C	85309
COLUMPIA RESORT	A	85610
EVI	C	85586
EVI A*	D	85586
FALIRAKI BAY*	C	85645
FALIRAKI BEACH	A	85301
FALIRO	E	85399
ERATO	B	85414
FIESTA	E	85498

Ialyssos (22410)

Hotel	Class	Tel
ALEXANDRA	D	91339
ALIA	B	31410
ANITA	C	94258
ANIXIS	C	91857
APOLLONIA	A	92951
ARGO SEA	B	90168
ARLEKINO	C	94490
BARBIE	C	95280
BARBIE II*	C	95280
BELAIR	A	23731
BELLE ELENE	B	92173
BENELUX	C	94011
BLUE BAY	A	91137
BLUE EYES	C	36797
BLUE HORIZON	A	93481
CARAVEL	A	94143
CAZA MANOS	D	94355
COSMOPOLITAN	A	35373
COSMOS	B	94080
D'ANDREA MARE*	A	96086
DEBBY	C	94651

Name	Cat	Tel
DIONYSOS	A	23021
EDEM	B	94284
EL DORANTO	C	94021
ELEKTRA PALACE	A	92521
ELENI	C	23050
ELEONAS	B	93791
ELINA	A	92466
FILERIMOS II	A	92510
FILERIMOS	A	92510
FILMAR	C	95313
FORUM	B	94321
FORUM BEACH*	A	96602
GALINI	B	94296
GOLDEN BEACH	A	92411
GOLDEN BEACH II	A	92411
HILTON RHODES RESORT	AA	75000
HIPPOCAMPUS	D	90206
IALYSOS CITY	B	95611
IALYSSOS BAY	A	91841
ISKAS	C	93205
IXIA	C	93557
KASSANDRA	B	94236
LATIN BEACH	A	94053
LE COCOTIERS	B	96450
LITO	B	23511
LIZA	C	96940
MARIBEL	A	94001
MARIETTAS' PARADISE	C	48209
MARITIME	C	92232
MARITINA	B	90501
METROPOLITAN KAPSIS	A	25015
MIRA-MARE WONDERLAND	A	96251
NATALIE	C	96691
NIKI	B	94065
OCEANIS	A	24881
OLYMPIC PALACE	A	28755
OSIRIS	A	94810
PACHOS	B	92514
PALEOS	A	92431
PALMASOL	C	93566
PEFKA	D	93533
POSEIDONI	AA	29000
POSEIDONIA II	A	29000
RHODIAN BEACH RESORT	A	89900
RHODOS PALACE	A	25222
ROMA	C	96447
RODINA'S APRTS	D	90081
SANTA HELENA	C	23301
SEA MELODY	A	91026
SOLEMAR	B	95290
SUMMER TIME	C	90100
SUMMER LAND	B	94941
SUN BEACH	A	93821
SUN BEACH II	A	91920
SUN OF RHODOS	C	94380
SUNDAY	C	91921
SUNNY DAYS	A	90006
SWAN	B	94502
TAKIS	D	92543
TASIMARI	C	94380
TERINIKOS	C	92174
KOTINOS	A	92454
VIVIAN	D	93515
WING	C	96361
LA ROSETA	B	92208
TRIANTA	C	94525
VERGINA	C	94386
ATLANTICA PRINCESS	A	92656
KATIA	D	94655
MATOULA BEACH	B	94251
MICHAEL	C	92691

Kremasti (22410)

Name	Cat	Tel
ALKYONIDES	D	95845
ANSELI	C	94633
ARMONIA	A	93077
EMERALD	C	90177
ESMERALDA	C	94469
GENNESIS	C	27649
KATSARAS	A	95004
KLADAKIS	C	91296
KREMASTI MEMORIES	C	96662
KREMASTI VILLAGE	A	92424
MARGARITA	C	94254
MATSIS	E	91064
MYRTO	D	93400
PILEA	B	92310
SUN FLOWER	B	93893
SUNLAND KREMASTI	B	91133
TSAPPIS	C	96764
VALENTINO	C	94631
VALSAMIS	A	98084
GREEN VIEW	D	91009

Theologos (22410)

Name	Cat	Tel
ALEX BEACH	A	82422
ALKMINI	B	42300
DORETTA BEACH	A	82540
HAPPY DAYS	B	82665
IFIGENIA	C	20310
IVORY	C	41679
NIRVANA BEACH	A	41127
SABINA	B	41635
STEVENSON	E	41557
SUMMER DREAM	B	41340

Name	Cat	Tel
MELITON	C	41666
ASTERIA	D	81902

Paradisi (22410)

Name	Cat	Tel
LIOS	C	94346
RHODIAN SUN	C	81945
SAVELEN	C	81855
VALLIAN VILLAGE	B	81127
VILLA HELENA	C	91175
GREEN VALLEY*	B	93040
MARAVELIA	C	81438

Kalavadra (22460)

Name	Cat	Tel
VOURAS	D	40003

Monolithos (22460)

Name	Cat	Tel
THOMAS	D	22741

Salakos (22460)

Name	Cat	Tel
NYMPFI	B	22206

Maritsa (22410)

Name	Cat	Tel
MIRA MONTE	E	47244

Pastida (22410)

Name	Cat	Tel
TOXOTIS	D	47691
GARDEN	C	47008

Archagelos (22440)

Name	Cat	Tel
AETHONAS	D	24185
ANAGROS	C	22248
ANTHI SUN	C	22619
ARHANGELOS	D	22230
CARAVOS	C	22961
CASTELO SUN	C	23190
FILIA	D	22604
HARAKI BAY	B	51680
KARYATIDES	C	22965
KATERINA	C	22169
MEANDROS	C	22896
NARKISSOS	C	22436
PHOEBUS	D	22600
PORTO ANGELI	A	24000
ROMANTIC	C	22749
ROSE MARIE	C	22263
SEMINA	C	22210
STELLA SUN	C	22978
TSAMPIKA SUN	C	22568

Afantou (22410)

Name	Cat	Tel
AFANTOU BEACH	B	51586
AFANTOU SKY	B	52347
CRYSTAL	C	51515
FILIPPOS	C	51933
GOLDEN DAYS	C	52302
GOLF VIEW	B	51935
GOLFER'S RESORT	C	27306

Name	Cat	Tel
IRIS	B	52233
LIPPIA HTL GOLF RESORT	A	52007
OASIS Bungalows Rhodes	A	51771
RENI SKY	B	51125
ROSE OF RODOS	C	52580
SCALA	C	51788
SIVILLA	B	51554
ST. NIKOLAS	D	51171
STAR VIEW	B	52100
YIANNIS	E	51565
KASTELI	D	51961

Kolympia (22410)

Name	Cat	Tel
ALFA	B	56411
ALFA BEACH*	A	56319
ALLEGRO	B	56286
DELFINIA REZORT	B	56601
DOUNAVIS	B	56212
EFKALYPTUS	E	56218
FANTASY	C	56485
GOLDEN ODYSSEY	A	56401
IRENE PALACE	A	56263
KOALA	B	56296
KOLYMPIA SKY	B	56271
KOLYMPIA BAY	B	56268
KOLYMPIA BEACH	A	56225
KOLYMPIA STAR	B	56419
KOLYMPIA SUN	C	51420
LOUTANIS	C	56312
LUTANIA BEACH	A	56295
LYDIA MARIS	A	56294
MARATHON	B	56380
MARY-ANNA PALACE	A	56466
MEMPHIS BEACH	B	56288
MISTRAL	B	56346
MYRINA BEACH	C	56254
NIRIIDES BEACH	A	56449
RELAX	B	56220
TINA FLORA	B	56251
TROPICAL	B	56279

Lindos (22440)

Name	Cat	Tel
AMPHITHEATER	B	31321
ATRIUM PALACE	A	31601
DANIEL	C	31584
EL VITA BEACH	C	44395
ELIOULA	B	44594
ELLI	E	31803
FILIMON	C	48158
FINAS	B	48107
KALATHOS SUN	D	31160
KALLIGA	C	31150
LINDOS AVRA	C	31376
LINDOS BAY	A	31501

LINDOS MARE	A	31130	CHRISTIANA	C	43228	SUN SHINE	C	44128	LE CHEF	D	6230
LINDOS MEMORIES	B	48153	DOLFIN	C	27172				PARADISE ROYAL		
LINDOS PINES	B	48259	EVAGELOS	C	43082	**Kiotari (22440)**			MAREA	A	6606
LINDOS STAR	B	31522	AMPELIA BEACH	B	43428	AEKATERINI	B	47048	PARADISE VILAGE	A	6704
LINDOS SUN	C	48270	GENNADI BAY	C	43194	KABANARIS BAY	C	47149	PEGASOS BEACH	A	8510
LYDIAN VILLAGE	B	47361	GENNADI SUN	C	43453	KIOTARI BAY*	A	47375	RODOS ROYAL	A	8549
MATINA PEFKI	B	48296	KAMINDOS	C	43100	KIOTARI BEACH	C	43521	SUNWING	A	8810
PALM BAY	C	48073	MARITA	C	43048	PRINCESS SUN	A	47105	VIRGINIA	B	6204
PEFKI ISLAND			OLYMPOS	C	43029	RODOS MARIS	A	47017	COLOSSOS BEACH	A	8552
RESORT	C	48181	PANORAMA			RODOS PRINCES	A	47102	OLYMPOS BEACH	A	8751
PEFKOS BEACH	B	48008	GENNADI	C	43315	RODOS VILLAGE	A	47201	PALLADIUM*	A	8600
PEFKOS VILLAGE			SUMMER BREEZE	C	43445	VILLA SYLVANA I	C	47167	LOMENIZ BLUE	B	6334
RESORT	B	48082	TINA'S	C	43340	VILLA SYLVANA II	C	47167			
STEPS OF LINDOS	A	31062							**Apolakia (22440)**		
STEPS OF LINDOS II	B	32000	**Lardos (22440)**			**Koskinou (22410)**			AMALIA	C	6136
SUMMER MEMORIES	C	48146	ANTONIS	D	44021	BLUE SEA	A	85582	SCOUTAS	E	6125
SUN GARDEN	B	31540	BELL MARE	B	44248	BLUE STAR	B	87640			
SUNRISE	B	48311	FEDRA	D	44213	CALYPSO	A	85623	**Lachania (22440)**		
THALIA	C	48249	ILYSSIO	C	48364	CALYPSO PALACE	A	85621	LACHANIA	D	4308
VILLE DI LINDOS	B	48260	KAMARI BEACH	A	44244	ESPERIDES	A	85525			
VLICHA SANDY			LARDOS BAY	B	44085	ESPEROS PALACE	A	85734	**Ladiko (22410)**		
BEACH	C	31042	LARDOS SUN BEACH	C	44203	ESPEROS VILLAGE	A	86046	LADIKO BUNGALOWS	A	8563
XENI	D	31171	LOSTAS	C	44141	ANKER	A	68149			
YIOTA	B	31605	MONTEMAR	B	44097	DOROTHEA	C	65134	**Kritika (22410)**		
ST. JOHN	B	44169	OLIVE GARDEN	C	44364	EDEN ROCK	A	67067	SIRENE BEACH	A	3065
			SMARA	C	44264	EPSILON	A	85912			
Genadi (24404)			ST. GEORGE	B	44203	CASTELLO	B	64856			
BETTY	C	3020	STAFILIA	B	47310	KRESTEN PALACE	A	64612			

Texts: T. PETRIS
Translation: PHILIP RAMP
Artistic editor: NORA ANASTASOGLOU
Photographs: M. TOUBIS S.A., A. PACHOS,
T. SPYROPOULOS, N. PASSALIS

Production - Printing: M. Toubis S.A.